DEVELOPING THE TEACHER IN YOU

DEVELOPING THE TEACHER IN YOU

WESLEY R. WILLIS

VICTOR BOOKS ®

A DIVISION OF SCRIPTURE PRESS PUBLICATIONS INC.
USA CANADA ENGLAND

Unless otherwise indicated, all Scripture quotations are from the *New American Standard Bible*, © The Lockman Foundation 1960, 1962, 1968, 1971, 1972, 1973, 1975, 1977. Other quotations are taken from the *Holy Bible, New International Version*, © 1973, 1978, 1984, International Bible Society. Used by permission of Zondervan Bible Publishers.

Library of Congress Cataloging-in-Publication Data

Willis, Wesley R.
    Developing the teacher in you/Wesley R. Willis
      p.   cm.
    ISBN 0-89693-040-8
    1. Christian education—Teacher training. 2. Christian education—Teaching methods. I. Title
    BV1533.W48 1990
    268.3—dc20   90-35255
                                                   CIP

---

1 2 3 4 5 6 7 8 9 10 Printing/Year 94 93 92 91 90

CONTENTS

INTRODUCTION

Excellence is a pleasure to observe in any area of life. Basketball fans delight to watch Michael Jordan drive the lane, launch himself toward the basket, and then complete one of his patented slam dunks. Even fans for the opposing team cheer Jordan in anticipation of a demonstration of excellence.

Music lovers sit enthralled as they listen to the excellence of Luciano Pavarotti singing an aria, or a concert organist performing a Bach fugue. And they signal their appreciation by applauding furiously, pleading for encore after encore.

One of the deceptive elements of such phenomenal excellence is the apparent ease with which the artists perform. Whether scoring baskets or singing arias, excellent performers give the impression that their achievements require little or no effort. By way of contrast, I recently observed a musician with little training and limited skill attempting to sing a moderately difficult song. As he groped for the high notes his neck tightened, his face turned red, and the vein in his forehead stood out. Many of us feared for his very health. Yet in spite of his obvious effort, the results were less than mediocre.

Teaching also can be an art form, reaching its ultimate expression in a consistent ministry of guiding students to grow spiritually. Just as in other expressions of excellence, many times the best teacher is the one who seems to perform with ease — leading the class by skillfully fielding questions, drawing out silent observers, and challenging students to strive to do their best.

Don't be deceived. Such excellence is the result of years of work and effort by the teacher. I once observed a professor who demonstrated unbelievable skill in writing on the chalkboard. Whenever he wrote a sentence, it always fit into the allotted space. His diagrams were clear and his charts were meticulously laid out. I longed to be able to write on the chalkboard with so little effort. Finally I asked him his secret. He explained that when no one was there he would come into the classroom to practice every chart, diagram, and sentence until it was exactly right. Yes, he possessed great skill. But his greatest asset was diligence in excellent preparation.

The purpose of this book is to help you become a better teacher than you are right now. Each chapter is divided into three sections. The first section, **Insight on Ministry,** deals with a specific aspect of excellence in teaching. Many of these sections first appeared as Christian education articles in *The Sunday School Planner*, published by Scripture Press.

The second section, **Insight from the Word,** will guide you through inductive study of several Scripture passages. You will need to use your Bible (preferably a New International Version) to answer the questions in this section. Each chapter divides the Bible study into two sections (Part One and Part Two). This is designed for study in two separate blocks of time during the week. If you are using the book for group study, the leader should subdivide the group and have some members study Part One while others study Part Two. Then in the larger meeting each group should share the results of their study with the other.

The final section, **Insight on Teaching,** suggests application of the principles covered in that chapter. This section provides material that can be studied in teacher training classes or reviewed privately. Follow through on the suggestions in this final section to build and refine your teaching skills.

Ideally, this book may be used to prepare a group of Sunday School teachers, or others, for their ministry in the local church. However, an individual can also use it just as effectively. If you do work through these studies alone, try to find another person who also wants to become a better teacher. Set up times to get together and discuss what you are learning. Excellence never is easy, it always comes as a result of time and work. There can be no higher calling than teaching another person the Word of God. If God has called you to use the gift of teaching, determine to give it the effort that it deserves. Do this and you will become an excellent teacher to the glory of God.

ONE

Teach Your Students; Don't Tell Them
(Teaching Without Manipulation)

Insight on Ministry

Recently I observed a teacher who had great problems controlling his class. He had prepared well and what he wanted to teach. He even employed creative methodology. And yet the class was rowdy and uncooperative. The teacher, anxious and frustrated, was considering dropping out of the teaching force.

Another person I know refused to even try teaching. She felt that she wasn't creative enough to keep the students' attention. The idea of, week after week, generating fresh and original ideas to maintain student interest proved to be a formidable barrier. And so she was not willing to attempt teaching. This teacher was a dropout even before she began. Her motto was, "It is better not even to try than to risk the chance of failure."

If you ever have tried to recruit teachers, you know the wide variety of excuses that you get. Some of them are similar to the excuses that Moses recited to God, recorded for us in chapters 3 and 4 of the Book of Exodus.

The purpose of the focus step is to redirect student attention away from the variety of individual interests toward the topic of the lesson. If I had known of the new toys, perhaps I could have planned a way to use them as a focus activity. (Unfortunately, I wasn't a fast enough thinker to figure out a way to do that on the spur of the moment.)

The focus phase of the lesson is when the attention of the students is directed toward the content to be learned. Unless students come together at this point, it becomes very difficult for the teacher to progress through the lesson. During this time the students are being prepared for what they are going to discover.

A variety of techniques can be employed for this purpose. Your curriculum materials should suggest focus activities designed to help the lesson get started. these could include illustrations, stories, questions, anecdotes, skits, role plays, visuals, and many other ideas. The prime qualifications for these activities is that they be attractive to the students and naturally lead into the discover phase of the lesson.

2. Discover

The second phase of the lesson is the discover phase. Once the students have become unified through the focus phase, they need to move on to learn the truth of God's Word. It is unfortunate that many curriculum materials available today merely masquerade as Bible-based materials. Sometimes this means that the lesson emphasis is a truth contained in the Bible. In other cases the materials may use Bible stories as a jumping-off point, with most of the lesson devoted to talking about good moral lessons rather than studying the inspired Word of God. These materials may refer to the Bible, but often neither the teacher nor the students need to use their Bibles. Good curriculum materials will include resources to help both teacher and student learn the facts of the Bible.

In Bible study, at least two things will be emphasized. The first is helping students learn the facts of the Bible. The actual Bible content is important; it is the biblical truth that God has promised to bless, and that students need to know. The second is helping students understand what those facts mean to them. This is the "personalization" of those facts. Curriculum materials should enable teachers to teach both the facts and the principles that apply to students' lives today.

The way that this is done is important. Few of us get very excited about being told what we ought to know. It is far more exciting to *discover* the truth for ourselves, thus we use the term to refer to this section of the lesson. It is a time when the student can perceive what God has said. Rather than the teacher telling them what is in the Bible, students should be able to discover it for themselves. Naturally the age level and maturity of the learner dictate the kind of discovery methods to be used and how much responsibility you can place upon the learner.

At the younger levels learners may discover meaning through the acting out or retelling of a Bible study. Older children may use their Bibles to seek answers to penetrating questions. Young people and adults may do inductive study or analyze key passages. They may start with a problem and seek biblical answers. Or they may begin with a passage and look for ways that it applies to everyday life.

However it is done, Sunday School and other Christian education programs need to move beyond the telling stage. Students must become active learners; they must discover truth themselves. Someone has said, "Give me a fish and you feed me for a day. Teach me how to fish, and you will feed me for a lifetime." This applies nowhere more than in Bible instruction. As we help learners discover Bible facts and principles, they are well along the way to becoming independent students of the Word.

3. Respond

The final phase of *Guided Discovery Learning* is when students begin responding to what they have learned. In a sense this is a discovery time, too, because students are discovering how they can apply biblical principles to life. Usually some sort of in-class activity is designed to get the students to begin applying what

15

they have discovered. If the principle discovered from the Bible directs us to show love to other Christians, students might begin by writing a letter in class to send to a sick class member. Later in the week they may visit that person in the hospital. They *begin* to respond in class, but the actual application should be a continuing experience, extending far beyond the class session.

This must be a guided time because few students will immediately know how to apply what has been learned. Instead, the teacher should be prepared with learning activities that will put the application process in motion. The time spent in class should help the learner take the first steps in applying Bible principles to life.

Guided Discovery Learning is not a novel or contemporary approach to teaching. We can find ample precedent in the teaching style of Jesus Christ. Repeatedly, He told the apostles only part of what they needed to know. Christ taught in such a way that they were stimulated to ask questions and seek answers themselves. He taught in parables and waited for them to ask for the interpretation. Sometimes He taught recognizing that they were confused, but knowing that they would grasp the meaning later. Also He sent them out to serve, knowing that they would encounter difficulties as they ministered. But He realized that they would return, more highly motivated than ever, seeking answers that only Christ could give.

Let's follow the Lord's model. Let's teach our students, and teach them well. But let's never confuse teaching with telling. Learners need to discover Bible truth for themselves. And we, as teachers, can guide them in that discovering. Then they will experience the satisfaction and joy of *Guided Discovery Learning.*

Insight from the Word (Part One)

Instead of recognizing that he did not have to be the "answer man" in order to minister effectively, Moses keenly felt the need to be in control. He did not want to become vulnerable and risk embarrassment. He did not want his lack of knowledge (either real or imagined) to be exposed. He was afraid that leading from a position of weakness would leave him open to rejection. And perhaps most of all, Moses was keenly aware of his lack of eloquence. He simply did not see himself as a public speaker—a leader.

Because he focused on these weaknesses—his supposed limitations—Moses felt that he could not serve God. But he forgot that ministry results come through the power of God, not through the power or capabilities of the servant. God called Moses and promised to work through him. But even as many people today may be reluctant to respond to God's call, Moses came up with all sorts of excuses why he could not do the job that God assigned to him. Let's look in detail at each of the four excuses that Moses gave to God.

EXCUSE NUMBER ONE: *"I'm not important enough (Ex. 3:11).* What can you observe in each of the following verses that would help to answer this first objection that Moses gave to God?

Exodus 3:8 (compare 3:10) _____

_____

(v. 10) _____

_____

(v. 12) _____

_____

How would the following verses contradict Moses' objections?

Exodus 2:14 _____

_____

(v. 15) _____

_____

How did the plan of Pharaoh (the equivalent of king/god in Egypt) described in Exodus 2:15 conflict with God's own plan recorded in Exodus 3:15? Overall, which of the plans should have had the greater impact, or been recognized as authoritative, and why?

_____

_____

_____

EXCUSE NUMBER TWO: "I don't know enough" (Ex. 3:13). How did God answer Moses' objection? (Ex. 3:14-17) _____

_____

_____

How did the simple statement at the beginning of Exodus 3:18 really answer all of Moses' fears about ignorance? _____

_____

_____

How did Exodus 3:21-22 further reinforce God's promise found in Exodus 3:10? _____

_____

_____

EXCUSE NUMBER THREE: "I'm not persuasive enough" (Ex. 4:1). What three signs did God promise that Moses could use to confirm his message? Exodus 4:2-5 _____

_____

(vv. 6-8) _____

_____

(v. 9) _____

_____

How did these answer Moses' protests over his inadequate powers of persuasion? _____

_____

_____

In what way did God's promise in Exodus 3:8 include all that Moses needed to answer this protest? _____

_____

_____

EXCUSE NUMBER FOUR: *"I'm not eloquent enough"* (Ex. 4:10). How did God answer this objection? (Ex. 4:11) _____

_____

_____

What promise did God make to Moses to encourage him? (Ex. 4:12) _____

_____

_____

What does Exodus 4:13 indicate to you about Moses' attitude toward the job that God had for him to do? _____

19

_____

_____

All of us who ever have taught have had fears, worries, or anxieties about teaching. Most of these relate to areas in which we feel inadequate for the task that God has called us to. In spite of Moses' reluctance, God revealed to us in Hebrews 11:23-29 that the real reason for Moses' success was his faith in God. This simply means that Moses trusted God. Today as we trust God, He will enable us to succeed in the same way.

Let's examine the concerns you might have about teaching. In the left column below list all of the fears and objections that you have about your teaching ministry. And then in the right column, list what you would like God to do to help you overcome the worries or limitations in the left column.

YOUR LIMITATIONS GOD WILL PROVIDE
_____

Insight from the Word (Part Two)

Once a person realizes that being a teacher does not mean having all the answers, much of the worry and anxiety is released. But a good teacher still has to know how to approach actually teaching the lesson. One of the easiest approaches is the one that follows the three-step sequence: (1) Focusing the attention of the students. (2) Helping students discover what God has given us in the Bible. (3) Encouraging students to respond to what God expects.

These three steps (Focus, Discover, and Respond) can be observed in Jesus' instruction as He ministered to the woman at the well of Sychar (John 4:7-30, 39-42). Read through the entire event at the well from John 4:7-42 and answer the following questions.

FOCUS: Consider how Jesus got the attention of the woman at the well of Sychar. What was His immediate need that Jesus used to focus her attention? (v. 7)

_____

_____

_____

How did Jesus stimulate her curiosity? (v. 10) _____

_____

_____

What was the woman's need that Jesus focused on? (v. 13)

_____

_____

DISCOVER: Consider the spiritual truths that Jesus taught the Samaritan woman. What did Jesus teach her about morality? (vv. 16-18) _____

_____

What did He teach her about worship, and about God's expectations for those who come to Him? (vv. 21-24) _____

_____

_____

What did Jesus reveal about Himself? (vv. 25-26) _____

_____

_____

RESPOND: Consider how the Samaritan woman acted upon the information that she discovered as Jesus taught her. What was her response in relation to others? (vv. 28-30) _____

_____

_____

What were the two reasons that others also responded to Jesus and His ministry? (v. 39) _____

_____

_____

(vv. 40-41) _____

_____

Insight on Teaching

Regardless of the age level of the students you are teaching, *Guided Discovery Learning* is an important concept. You first must gain the students' attention and focus on common needs that they have. Then you will be able to teach them what God has communicated through His Word. Next, they will discover important truths. Finally, effective teaching concludes with a specific response that is a natural outgrowth of the Bible lessons that students discovered.

TEACHING CHILDREN: Most teachers of children can identify specific responses that they desire from their students. But often the problem is getting class attention, and then helping them discover truths that are relevant to that particular age level. We tend to plunge right into the lesson, and yet we may not have spent adequate time focusing their attention. Remember to listen to class members, both in class and outside of it. They will talk about the things that interest them. These things can become good starting points for focusing your lessons.

Most lessons for younger children are designed to help them discover truth through Bible stories. Preschool and early elementary lessons will approach discovery through stories while older elementary ones may concentrate on the characters themselves. The *Respond* time is extremely important, with various learning activities, handcrafts, guided play, in-class workbooks, and projects all designed to help children understand and apply the lesson to their lives during the week. Take-home papers are an important tool in reinforcing both *Discover* and *Respond* times from the lesson.

TEACHING YOUTH: Teachers of youth need to spend significant time in *Focus* activities. This is an excellent time to build rapport with class members. This means listening to and chatting with them about their interests. Informal, casual discussion is not wasted time, rather, it lays the foundation for later discovery of truth. Not only is it important to listen in class, but teachers of youth should look for ways to spend time with students outside of class. Find out what they think, what activities occupy their time, and where their interests lie.

When you guide youth in discovering truth, it is very important to encourage discussion — interactive methods. Try not to lecture too much of the time, but instead ask them questions. And encourage them to ask you questions. In this way they will participate actively in discovering truth. Be sure to let them know that no question is out of bounds. And don't worry if you don't have all the answers. Remember, no teacher in the world has all the answers. But when you don't know an answer, be sure to check with your pastor or other authority to help find a good response to share in the next session.

TEACHING ADULTS: One of the main traps that most adult teachers fall into is the lecture orientation. Somehow we assume that the way to teach adults is to tell them what the Bible says and then tell them what they ought to do because of it. It is far better to use methods that will allow class members the privilege of discovering what God has given us in His Word. This means using interactive methods to teach. Excellent methods for adults include question/answer, discussion, inductive study, and any other strategies that cause students to think, talk, or actively participate in learning activities. When such methods are used, adults will discover far more than when we simply tell them what the Bible says. And, they will have a much higher level of interest, retention, and application too.

TWO

7 Steps to Better
Lesson Preparation
(A Painless Way to Get Ready to Teach)

Insight on Ministry

"Could I teach these curriculum materials if I walked into Sunday School and was handed the teaching guide, informed that the teacher didn't show up? Would I be able to take that guide and, without any preparation, teach the lesson?" Those questions were put to me by a person wanting to know more about the Sunday School curriculum materials we were discussing.

His question reminded me of how I felt after a twenty-five hour trip to India where I was to conduct a series of Christian education seminars. I arrived at 1 A.M. Wednesday (which felt like 2 P.M. Tuesday) after leaving home at 1 P.M. Monday. I was both exhausted and hungry. But which drive was stronger? If I stayed up and ate, I would become even more tired. But if I went right to bed, I still would be hungry and might have trouble getting to sleep. I struggled with conflict because whichever drive I satisfied would leave the other need unfulfilled.

I experienced a similar conflict when queried about teaching

25

without preparation. As a Christian educator, I know the importance of quality study time, and didn't want to imply that any publisher would encourage teaching without preparation. No person can teach effectively by coming in cold to the lesson, picking up a teaching guide and trying to lead a class in meaningful learning. Before using that approach there are far better options to suggest. But I knew that my questioner would not accept these alternatives. He wanted an answer to his question. There was no escape; I had to provide an answer.

So we decided to see if it could be done. We picked up a teaching guide and started to read aloud. We found that some activities needed to be prepared, or materials had to be gathered ahead of time. But there were alternatives that worked. And while it might not have been a very good lesson, it certainly could have been taught — cold. Even as I reiterated that we never would encourage or even suggest such a thing, we found out that it is possible. This discovery met both of my desires — to encourage good preparation and to show how easy it is to teach the Sunday School curriculum materials in question.

The questioning encounter started me thinking about the entire process of lesson preparation. Over the years I have taught most age groups in the church, from toddlers to senior citizens. Some things work for me, and others don't. My preparation probably differs from yours. And yet a systematic approach to preparation greatly simplifies the task. The following steps are appropriate for a teacher to follow in getting ready to teach most published Sunday School curriculum materials.

STEP ONE: PRAY FOR YOUR STUDENTS. This precedes the actual preparation. A good teacher will spend time praying for specific student needs. In addition to the direct benefit of prayer, you also reap the side benefits of becoming more sensitive to student needs as well as getting to know them better.

One tool I have found helpful in this area is preparing a notebook for guidance in praying for class members. Assign one page to each student. In the first section record basic information such as name, address, phone number, birthday, place of school or work, and other family members. In a second section, record information about any special interests or skills of that student. Devote the third section to prayer requests for that person, including space to record answers to prayer.

Not only will you minister to your students as you pray through the list, but you will think about them and their needs as you prepare to teach. And there's another value too. In order to fill out the information, you need to talk to a student in depth. Meet with each student alone long enough to get information to fill out the sheet. You will learn about your students, and begin building close relationships. And they will recognize that you really care for them as individuals.

STEP TWO: READ THE ASSIGNED SCRIPTURE PASSAGE(S). Studying the teaching guide is not the best way to begin preparation. But you do need to check the guide to find the assigned passage for the week. Then spend some time reviewing the Bible. If you begin early in the week, you can read through the passage several times before you actually do your formal class preparation.

As you read through the passage take note of several things. Write down any questions that occur to you as you read. Perhaps you are studying the account of Jesus and the Samaritan woman by the well of Sychar (John 4:1-42). You might ask yourself, "Who are the Samaritans? And why did the Jews have no dealings with them?" (v. 9) You might wonder what a well looked like, or where the city of Sychar (v. 5) was located. These are questions that you will need to answer, perhaps from the teaching guide.

You also should write down key ideas that the passage contains. These should be main ideas or concepts that seem to be taught in the text. Your goal is to get an idea of what the passage is all about. As you better understand it you will begin to see how its main ideas apply to the specific needs of your class members.

STEP THREE: GET A LESSON OVERVIEW. Now you are ready to begin looking into the teacher's guide. What are the title and the theme of the lesson? How do these fit into any unit theme? Look at the aims of the lesson. These always should include both a content aim (Bible knowledge) and a behavior aim (life response). Note the memory or key verse. Do you know that verse? If not, begin to work on memorizing it. The teacher benefits from Bible memorization, and it is an excellent example for the students too.

The Bible is the crucial element in developing and communicating any Sunday School lesson. We need to help our students become what God wants them to be with the Bible as our source of authority. And in order for them (and us) to do what God wants us to do, we need to know the facts of the Bible. This means a commitment to Bible memorization and mastery of Bible stories. We need to know what God has communicated.

But true learning involves more than acquiring facts. It includes a change in behavior, a life response. Jesus explained the danger of merely hearing His words and doing nothing about them in the Parable of the House on the Rock. "I will show you what he is like who comes to Me and hears My words and puts them into practice. He is like a man building a house, who dug down deep and laid the foundation on rock. When a flood came, the torrent struck that house but could not shake it, because it was well built. But the one who hears My words and does not put them into practice is like a man who built a house on the ground without a foundation. The moment the torrent struck that house, it collapsed and its destruction was complete" (Luke 6:47-49, NIV). If we teach Bible facts but ignore application, we may contribute to future failure when students face difficult circumstances.

You are finally ready to begin studying the lesson after learning the title, Scripture passage, memory verses, and both Bible knowledge and life response aims. For your convenience, most publishers group these, and other related elements, together at the beginning of the lesson.

STEP FOUR: READ THROUGH THE TEACHING GUIDE. This step is one that many teachers omit. And obviously you still can do a fine job without it. But I find it helpful to take a few minutes to read through the entire lesson before beginning to study any specific section. This gives one a good overview of the lesson development. It lets you see how the parts are intended to fit together after the lesson is all prepared.

STEP FIVE: STUDY THE BODY OF THE LESSON. This section is the heart of the lesson. While various publishers have different names for it, this is the part that deals with Bible content. You need to use your own Bible, and study from it, but you also will utilize the teaching guide resource. A teacher's guide is a Bible commentary, Bible dictionary, concordance, and educational guide combined with a variety of other resources. Curriculum writers and editors have combed through many resources and selected what they feel will be most helpful in studying the lesson and planning learning activities.

In studying the body of the lesson students should learn the facts of the Word of God. As you study the lesson make sure it teaches what the Bible passage emphasizes. Sometimes there may be several potential lessons from the same text. You may need to select the one that best relates to your class. Feel free to modify and adapt the teaching guide if necessary, but always make sure that your emphasis derives from a correct interpretation of the Bible passage.

Methods are a very important part of this section. It is all too easy to think that because we are teaching the *Word,* we need to use *words* — to lecture. When we teach the Bible our goal ought to be helping students to discover its truth. This means that a variety of methods should be used. Be sure to consult the student guide at this point in your preparation to see the assigned activities that learners will be doing.

STEP SIX: STUDY THE APPLICATION SECTION. Application ought to flow naturally out of the previous section. While various publishers identify the section by different names, this part of the lesson is where the life response aim is emphasized. It answers the "so what?" question that good students ask. While it is imperative that first we know Bible facts, it also is important to recognize the implication of those facts for everyday living. In many lessons you will have a choice of alternative applications and learning activities to help achieve the life re-sponse aim. Be sure to select those that relate most directly to your students.

Study the student guide as well as the teacher's guide. This will help you take advantage of the varied activities designed to maximize application. Even though the publisher has selected passages of Scripture that deal most directly with the particular age group that you are teaching, you must individualize the lesson. Personalize the application based on the needs you per-ceive from the time you have spent listening to and observing your students.

STEP SEVEN: STUDY THE INTRODUCTION SECTION. To some people this may seem out of place. Why do I suggest studying the introduction last? Because I find it far easier to plan the introduction after I know what it is I am trying to introduce. Anytime you begin teaching a lesson, you face the task of taking students with wide-ranging interests and directing them to the Word of God. We must assume that they don't come into class motivated to learn. Almost without exception, a student's attention is elsewhere. But well-chosen activities can move students from diverse, individual interests and draw their attention to the lesson of the day.

Most publishers offer alternative introduction suggestions. Consider all the options presented. Perhaps you will come up with effective ideas not mentioned in the materials. Let your creativity soar. Try some things that you never have tried be-fore. But be sure that the introductory activities move the stu-dents *toward* the learning aims and not away from them.

It is helpful to study the student guide to understand the meaningful introductory activities it provides. This also is the time to consider presession activities for those who arrive early. Ideally they should lead into the focus activities. Finally, consid-er how any group activities (opening or closing worship) for several classes combined might integrate with what you will be doing in your own class.

These seven steps will not solve all teaching problems, but they will systematize your study to help you derive maximum value. While it is true that some teachers could walk into class with little or no preparation and do an acceptable job, I don't recommend it. The quality of preparation influences the quality of instruction. But preparation doesn't have to be tedious. Following these seven simple steps will remove much of the "pain" from preparing to teach your lesson.

Insight from the Word (Part One)

Jesus taught many things through parables, which many of us learned in Sunday School are "earthly stories with heavenly meanings." Even though they require some interpretation, ordinarily the meaning is fairly obvious. Perhaps one of the most important principles to keep in mind when examining a parable is not to take the meaning *too* far. Usually there are a few main ideas that Jesus taught through any given parable.

One of the very important lessons on discipleship that Jesus taught was communicated through a series of brief parables. These can be found in Luke 14:26-33 and often are grouped under the general heading of "Counting the Cost," or "The Demands of Discipleship." This series is somewhat unique in that Jesus spoke a basic principle (Luke 14:26-27), followed by two very brief parables (vv. 28-30 and vv. 31-32), with a restatement of the basic principle (v. 33). This simplifies interpretation for us because Jesus Himself explained what the parables meant.

PRINCIPLE: Jesus demands absolute commitment (which He can do because He is God) from His followers. Many have struggled with the statement in Luke 14:26 (NIV), "If anyone comes to Me and does not hate his father and mother, his wife and children, his brothers and sisters — yes, even his own life — he cannot be My disciple." Obviously Jesus was not advocating rejection and/or a dislike of relatives. If this were so, then hating one's own life logically would lead to suicide, which we know Jesus did not advocate. Matthew 10:37 clarifies that Jesus was concerned with comparative allegiance. He requires absolute allegiance. He has to have first place in the mind of a disciple. All others, even self, must take second place behind that primary commitment to the Lord.

Luke 14:27 extends this principle to our own personal lives and drives. These also are to fall in line behind Jesus. Carrying a cross was identified with a person who was about to die. It demonstrated that the one carrying it had absolutely no control over his own life. And even as Jesus, on the way to the cross, demonstrated His willingness to give up His own preferences (Matt. 26:42), so His disciples must demonstrate the same attitude.

At the end of this section (Luke 14:33) following the two brief parables, Jesus reiterated the principle. Genuine disciples must relinquish independent exercise of their will and resources to the direction of the Master, Jesus Christ. Relationships, time, possessions, skills — all must be given to Him if we wish to serve as true disciples.

PARABLES: In your own words, briefly summarize the main ideas (the earthly story) of the parable in Luke 14:28-30.

_____

_____

_____

_____

_____

In light of the principle stated before and after this parable, what do you think Jesus was trying to teach through this particular parable? _____

_____

_____

Why would such a message be important to a follower of Jesus?

_____

_____

_____

The other parable relating to Jesus' teaching is in Luke 14:31-32. Summarize its main ideas. _____

_____

_____

_____

_____

_____

How does this parable reinforce the same message that was taught in the previous one? _____

_____

_____

If you are teaching a class, you have made a commitment to allocate time and energy to that task. What are some of the conflicting demands that could make it inconvenient to teach a class? _____

_____

_____

_____

How might the message of these parables apply to you and your teaching ministry? _____

_____

_____

_____

_____

_____

How do you expect to handle the tensions that arise from such conflicts? _____

_____

_____

_____

_____

_____

Insight from the Word (Part Two)

Another parable that Jesus taught is recorded in Matthew 7:24-27. In this brief parable, Jesus recounted the events surrounding two building projects. In one, a man built his house on a rock. When the elements struck, it remained solidly in place. The second man built his on sand. Under the assault of the same elements, his house collapsed with a crash. The chart below lists the various elements of the parable. Fill in the blank application sections (how you can personalize this passage in your life) based on your understanding of the meaning of the parable.

Features	Wise Man	Application	Foolish Man	Application
Foundation	Rock	_____	Sand	_____
Elements	Rain	_____	Rain	_____
	Flood	_____	Flood	_____
Results	Stability	_____	Collapse	_____

In what ways might the application of this parable relate to your teaching ministry? Since there always is the possibility of teaching without applying the truth of the Word of God, what dangers or cautions might be relevant to Bible teachers?

_____

_____

_____

_____

How can you plan your teaching approach to avoid the possibility that students might fail to apply the lessons that you teach?

_____

_____

_____

Insight on Teaching

TEACHING AT ALL LEVELS: Make photocopies of the Student Information Sheet on page 37 (or design your own similar forms) so you have one to fill out for each student in your class.

Complete these sheets and use them as you pray for your students and as you prepare to teach your class each week. Use additional sheets for prayer requests and answers if you find that you run out of room.

Some teachers have found it helpful to take photographs of their students to attach to the information sheet as they begin each new year. Be sure to let your students know why you are taking the photos and how you intend to use them. It will help them to appreciate their importance to you.

TEACHING CHILDREN: Once you have recorded the names of the students in your class, there are several things you should do to teach them more effectively. Don't forget to call each of their parents. Try to learn as much as you can about each individual student. This will help you to fill out the information sheets. Be sure to let the parents know that you are genuinely interested not only in teaching their children, but in helping them with their task of rearing their children.

Once you have compiled a sheet on each class member, draw up a list of the general problems or needs that your class members must face. While many of these will be common to learners of that particular age level, you may also find some that are unique to your class due to geographical location, the nature of the local school system, employment rates in the area, etc. Supplement this list by reading about the developmental stages of the children that you teach. If your church library doesn't have books on age characteristics, consult with the publisher of your curriculum materials to find some recommended books to help you. You also can get good information in the developmental psychology section of your local library.

After you compile this problems/needs list, refer to it periodically as you prepare. Be sure to apply the Word of God, as you are teaching it, to these needs. Remember the importance of application as well as the danger of knowing truth and failing to act upon it (James 1:22; 3:1).

TEACHING YOUTH: It is important for you to talk to your teens directly in getting to know their needs. You might devise a

STUDENT INFORMATION SHEET

NAME _____

ADDRESS _____

_____

PHONE _____

BIRTHDAY _____

SCHOOL/WORK _____

_____   (photo)

_____

FAMILY MEMBERS _____

_____

_____

SPECIAL INTERESTS _____

_____

_____

PRAYER REQUESTS _____ ANSWERS _____

_____   _____

_____   _____

_____   _____

_____   _____

brief questionnaire to assist in this task. Ask them to list things such as their favorite musical groups or sports activities, what they like to do in their spare time, and what they like to read for pleasure. Becoming acquainted with their music and magazines will help you to better understand them. As you gain their confidence, and can assure them that their answers will be kept confidential, try asking more probing questions. You might ask, "What do you like most about yourself?" and "What would you change about yourself if you could?" These will help you to gain insight for applying Bible truth to their lives.

In the weeks following the questionnaire, meet with each student privately with the intent of better getting to know each other. Explain that you want to fill out an information sheet so that you can pray more intelligently for each one of them. Listen carefully to what the teen says as you talk together. This time spent together will be most helpful in building a basic relation-ship, and it will give you the chance to follow up with later informal meetings throughout the year. You also will be able to get an update on answers to prayer and on current prayer needs.

TEACHING ADULTS: You will need to interview each class member in order to fill out the information sheet. If your class is large, you might have to resort to collecting the information over the phone. It is preferable to meet each one (or married couple) personally and individually to secure the information. Be sure to explain what you are doing and why you want the information. Encourage your students to contact you when they need prayer for special situations. Remember to follow up to find out the status of special prayer requests.

Once you have filled out an information sheet for each stu-dent, make a chart listing the primary occupations of those in your class. These could include categories such as executive, factory worker, salesperson, homemaker, student, etc. Under each of these categories, list the basic needs that you have discovered about the class members. Periodically update this chart, and review it each week as you begin to prepare to teach. This will help to maintain relevancy in your teaching and pro-mote effective application of the Bible truths that you teach.

THREE

Guiding Students
Effectively
(What You Are Is as Important as What You Do)

Insight on Ministry

Our family has many delightful memories from camping trips through the years. One particular trip, several years ago, stands out in my memory. Elaine and I, along with our three sons, Mark, Kevin, and Nathan, spent almost a week canoeing the Boundary Waters area of northern Minnesota. This wilderness area is ideally suited for such activities. Though natural and unspoiled, it is well-mapped and relatively safe (just don't ask Elaine about the bear!). Because trips into the Boundary Waters are not particularly hazardous, most groups do not need a guide. With a reliable outfitter, good maps, and some wilderness proficiency, competent canoeists can handle the experience.

However, other areas demand professional guides. Recently I spent several weeks speaking in Alaska, where both common sense and the law require that outsiders hire a guide for wilderness activities. Imagine that we are about to explore one of those dangerous areas. The guide, whom we have not yet met, arrives to greet us. After exchanging introductions, he begins to speak of the wilderness beyond. He tells us how beautiful he has heard that it is. True, many potential dangers exist, but he hopes that we will not encounter any since he has no first-aid supplies. By the time our alleged guide asks us if anyone in the group has a map and compass that he can borrow, the picture has become very clear. This man is not qualified to be a member of our group, let alone to guide us. Needless to say, our plans would change on the spot. If we still wanted to explore the area, we would hire another guide. No group wants a guide who is inexperienced, unskilled, and unprepared.

In many ways, a teacher is similar to a guide. A guide must know the area to be explored before helping others discover that region. Both guide and teacher must be well prepared to handle unexpected situations. Ultimately, the guide's value is in providing others with a proper experience. Likewise, a teacher's activities take on meaning only as learners have positive experiences that help to produce desired results. Learning is an activity that teachers can encourage and promote, but teachers cannot learn for their students. Students must learn and develop for themselves, encouraged and enabled by the activities of the teacher.

One of the questions that I regularly discuss in teacher seminars that I conduct is how teaching is similar to other vocations such as policeman, lecturer, news commentator, sculptor, and guide. Participants then vote on which they think is most like teaching. Usually sculptor and guide receive the most votes. Obviously guide is a good choice for the reasons we considered earlier. But the choice of sculptor is in my opinion unfortunate. Unfortunate because this implies that the teacher's work is what really matters. True, teaching involves an element of sculpting, but not because a teacher serves as sculptor. Rather the true sculptor is God, and a teacher is the tool in God's hand.

A teacher may draw erroneous conclusions if he or she perceives the task of teaching from a sculptor's viewpoint. Such thinking suggests that a teacher has absolute authority over the outcome of the teaching/learning process. We all know that this is not the case. Students have minds of their own and must make their own decisions. While the teacher certainly can play a significant role by guiding the learner toward good decisions, each learner, led by God's Holy Spirit, ultimately must decide personally.

Another implication of the "teacher as sculptor" school of thought is that every teacher would need absolute knowledge. In order to play such a determinative role a teacher would have to precisely know each student's potential and how to develop it. Understandably, some prospective teachers feel intimidated by this suggestion. But any teacher should recognize that he or she does not, in fact, need profound insight or manipulative ability. A teacher is not a sculptor. Our omniscient God is the sculptor, and the teacher should be His tool.

In the final analysis, teaching might be described most accurately as "an activity that promotes learning." Of course a teacher can do this only if he or she continues to learn also. A teacher who is discovering God's truth and applying it personally is in a position to help others learn. Rather than being the source of all wisdom and knowledge, a teacher's prime obligation is to guide students through the teaching/learning process. The student's responsibility is to learn. And God expects a teacher to help each student learn, even as that teacher has been learning and applying God's truth.

Guiding Through Example

Unquestionably, the most significant way in which a teacher guides students is through personal example. The very character of a teacher influences learners, whether the teacher serves as parent, church leader, or some other significant role model.

A young mother asked a well-known Bible teacher when she ought to start teaching her children about God. The teacher answered, "About twenty years before your baby is born." His point was that what we are teaches our children far more than what we say. Parents serve as models for children. But if there is discrepancy between what parents say and what they do, children usually imitate what the parents do.

Teachers also teach by modeling, which is the reason that Paul challenged Timothy to live a godly life — to teach by example: "Command and teach these things. Don't let anyone look down on you because you are young, but set an example for the believers in speech, in life, in love, in faith, and in purity" (1 Tim. 4:11-12, NIV).

Teachers must first be what they would teach, which is why a teacher who is not a learner cannot be a good teacher. Only as we learn the lessons that God teaches us can we serve as models for our students. Teachers guide students and demonstrate truth in action for them by modeling Christian living.

Jesus Christ's earthly ministry lasted only three years. In that brief time, His challenge was to take a small group of individuals with diverse backgrounds and knowledge and to equip them for the most important task that a handful of men ever would be asked to accomplish. And He did.

Modeling was a vital part of the teaching ministry of Christ. "And He went up to the mountain and summoned those whom He Himself wanted, and they came to Him. And He appointed twelve, that they might be with Him, and that He might send them out to preach" (Mark 3:13-14). Notice that Christ planned for the disciples to be with Him. While the Twelve learned from the Lord's spoken instruction, the personal time that they spent with Him was equally important. As they watched Him minister, they developed an awareness that went far beyond the actual words that they heard. They came to love and follow their Master. And as that happened, their ministry skills developed too. They were taught by who and what Christ was as well as by what He said.

Jesus' approach means building personal relationships with learners so that they actually incorporate qualities of the teacher into their own lives. The goal is for the students to learn to minister to others even as the teacher is ministering to them. As Christ was developing His followers, He explained the impact of true teaching in Luke 6:40 (NIV): "A student is not above his teacher, but everyone who is fully trained will be like his teacher."

And this is what happened in Christ's ministry. His disciples lived with Him, learned from Him, and became like Him. Jesus' character and commitment had a transforming effect on eleven of His twelve followers. And in the years following His resurrection, this small group of disciples turned the world upside down. We live and serve Christ today because of the impact of their ministry and those who followed.

The Apostle Paul also guided those whom he taught. He encouraged the believers at Philippi and Corinth to model their lives after his example and after other Christian teachers whom they had known: "Join with others in following my example, brothers, and take note of those who live according to the pattern we gave you" (Phil. 3:17, NIV).

At about this point some of you probably are contemplating turning in your "teacher" badge and offering to bake brownies for the youth group instead. But wait! Guiding through example does not demand that we teachers must be perfect. If that were the case, there would be no teachers. None of us would qualify.

What guiding through example does demand is openness and honesty. We know that we are not perfect. And so do our students. Guiding through example means that we represent ourselves as we are — Christians in the process of becoming. We struggle with temptation. We lose our tempers. We fail. But when we miss the mark, we can provide an example to our students by dealing positively and biblically with our shortcomings.

Demonstrating the proper way to deal with failure is a significant part of guiding. I know of one youth leader who lost his temper because all of the young people were laughing at him. But losing his temper was not the real failure. His greater mistake was failing to admit that he had done wrong and that he needed to ask forgiveness. Instead he stubbornly resisted admitting error. And within months he resigned due to the students' loss of respect.

The young people didn't demand that this youth worker be perfect — they knew what failure was and that leaders make mistakes too. But they did expect him to correct his error. Even his failure could have been turned into positive guidance if only he had been willing to model the proper way to deal with sin.

It is important to recognize that the true impact of teaching extends beyond content. We certainly must never demean the importance of content, but the message of truth cannot be separated from the person who communicates that truth. The Bible is God's true and accurate revelation. But in order to teach it most effectively, that revealed truth from God must be demonstrated and reflected through the life of the instructor. This was the case in the ministry of Jesus Christ. It was true in the teaching of Paul, and it continues in our ministries today.

Guiding Through Methods

Another technique of guiding learners to consider is the use of appropriate methodology. At workshops I frequently ask participants to describe what a teacher *should* be most like. Virtually no one ever suggests a lecturer. But when I ask what *is* the most common teaching method, invariably the answer is "lecture."

Curiously, we know that lecture is not the most effective way to teach, and yet it is the method of choice. We know that teachers should guide their students into learning. Yet we neglect the methods that will promote meaningful learning — methods that enable students to explore and discover truth for themselves.

Some years ago, I chaired a college Christian Education department. One of the tracks in the CE major was camping ministry. And one of the courses was wilderness ministry. The goal of this course was to help students learn how to minister effectively in the out-of-doors, specifically in wilderness contexts. I had taken a similar course as a student. Believe it or not, the entire course was conducted inside the four walls of the classroom. We never even went outside onto the campus!

As I was preparing to teach wilderness camping, the absurdity of my own experience struck me — being lectured to about outdoor experiences. And so I determined not merely to lecture, but to guide my class into learning. Our class consisted of learning how to prepare for wilderness experiences and then actually participating in a wilderness camping trip.

This is not to say that there were no lectures. I used a variety of teaching methods. Sometimes it was important to give content. Those lectures served to prepare the students to actually participate in a wilderness experience.

Guiding learners should be the underlying strategy in all of our teaching. While we certainly want to present biblical content in an interesting manner, ultimately we should try to help students become active learners. Doing this will mean choosing methods and planning activities that secure active learner involvement. We should emphasize activities that will get students digging into God's Word for themselves. They should interact, discuss, and dramatize — always participating actively.

As you prepare your lesson, select those methods suggested in your teacher guide that get students involved in the learning process. Don't concentrate on just presenting information, but plan interactive methods. View yourself as a guide — as one who enables discovery learning to take place. And as you emphasize *Guided Discovery Learning,* your students will come alive. They will learn and they will learn to love it.

Teachers have been called many things — both good and bad. But the most flattering comment that could be made about a teacher is to describe him or her as a guide. The teacher who approaches instruction as one guiding learners is the teacher who will be effective. We must guide through our lives remembering that the attitudes and actions of teachers influence students immeasurably. We must plan to use methods that will promote active student involvement — methods that will help students to discover God's truth. When we teach in this way, students will learn and grow through *Guided Discovery Learning.*

Insight from the Word (Part One)

A young father walking through a park was followed by his toddling son. It was interesting to observe the son as he followed his father. If the father swatted at a bug, the son also swatted an imaginary bug. When the father stretched to take a longer step over an obstacle, the son also stretched to step. When the father reached down to pick up a stone and throw it, his son picked up a stone and attempted the same. Whatever the father did, his son mimicked him.

Such imitation is not limited to fathers and sons; all parents exert influence over their children. Children will imitate what they see their parents doing. Unfortunately, this goes for undesirable traits as well as those that we want them to emulate. In fact, what parents *do* exerts a far more powerful influence than what they *say*. Studies demonstrate that when there is a contradiction between what parents tell their children to do and what the parents actually do, the children most commonly follow the example not the verbal instruction.

A similar relationship exists between teacher and student. While it is important that teachers speak the truth, it is even more important that they live the truth. We often refer to this as modeling — demonstrating the truth through the way that we live. Read Luke 6:40. What does this verse suggest about the importance of the modeling that a teacher does? _____

_____

_____

How does Luke 6:39 contribute to our understanding of this principle? _____

_____

_____

_____

Think back to an outstanding teacher — one whom you greatly admired. What stands out in your memory of that teacher?

_____

_____

_____

Often we fall into the trap of thinking that a teacher's skill in using effective methods is most important. What does Luke 6:40 suggest about the importance of character? _____

_____

_____

_____

Read Philippians 3:17. In addition to Paul, who served as models for the Philippian Christians? _____

_____

_____

How were the Philippians, who were learning how to live as Christians, supposed to relate to Paul and the other models?

_____

_____

Observe what Paul wrote in Philippians 3:12-14. He obviously was keenly aware of the fact that he had not "arrived" at the pinnacle of spiritual maturity. What evidence do you find of Paul's humility in verse 12? _____

_____

What additional evidence do you observe in verse 13? _____

_____

_____

_____

What was Paul's objective in life according to verse 14?

_____

_____

How might the message of Luke 6:39-40 influence your understanding of and approach to your teaching ministry? _____

_____

_____

_____

_____

How might Paul's example of his exhortation to follow those who are living as good examples influence how your preparation for a ministry of teaching? _____

_____

_____

_____

_____

Insight from the Word (Part Two)

Often we draw a parallel between parenting children and teaching students. Many of the same dynamics influence both activities. Paul often referred to those whom he taught as his children in the Lord. And he described his ministry as one of relating to those whom he taught both as mother and as father (1 Thes. 2:7, 11-12).

One of those followers whom Paul taught was Timothy. Timothy was a relatively young man who had traveled and ministered with Paul and who had been trained by Paul in ministry skills. Paul stressed the importance of modeling Christian character as an effective teacher in his letter to Timothy (1 Tim. 4:11-12). When Paul wrote this, Timothy may well have been the young pastor of the church at Ephesus. In any event, he was responsible to teach his students faithfully and effectively. And this included modeling.

Read 1 Timothy 4:11-12. Below in the left column, list the five qualities through which Timothy could be an example (model) to the believers. In the right column, list specific actions or behaviors which allow those qualities to be seen by a teacher's students. The first of the five is completed as an example.

QUALITIES	PRACTICAL DEMONSTRATION
1. SPEECH	*I should be careful not to say unkind things about others.*
	I must avoid gross or obscene language.
	I will compliment my students.
2. _____	_____

49

_____

_____

3. _____ _____

_____

_____

_____

_____

4. _____ _____

_____

_____

_____

_____

5. _____ _____

_____

_____

_____

_____

_____

How would you feel about having a teacher who demonstrated the positive qualities in the lists above and who also avoided the negative ones? _____

_____

_____

What do you think that you need to do to cultivate those positive qualities in your own life? _____

_____

_____

_____

_____

What might hinder you from being a good example to your students and modeling appropriate Christian behavior? _____

_____

_____

_____

_____

Take a few minutes right now to pray asking God to help you avoid those things that might hinder good modeling and build up those qualities that will enhance your life and ministry.

Insight on Teaching

TEACHING CHILDREN: Children often form very strong opinions about whether or not a teacher likes them. Many times these opinions are based on the level of warmth and friendliness exhibited by the teacher. Be sure that you genuinely love those children whom you teach, and then look for ways to communicate that love. Even though some children may act in ways that you might not find attractive, ask God to give you a genuine love for each one. And then work hard at communicating this love through smiles, affirmation, encouragement, and other specific ways that say, "You are special and I love you."

Children are extremely sensitive to how fair things are. They have a highly idealized view of fairness; and if they feel that they are not being treated equally children will take this as evidence of rejection. If you want to model the love and acceptance of Jesus to your students, you must seek to treat them fairly. Don't single out one to help you all of the time. Be sure to pass the "privilege" around.

TEACHING YOUTH: It is fairly obvious that if a teacher is to be a strong personal influence to young people, that teacher has to be in contact with them. This is one reason why activities outside of the formal teaching time are so valuable. They provide the contacts for the informal relationships that often develop into significant guidance opportunities. Sometimes sitting next to a young person at a sporting event will provide more meaningful discussion opportunities than a year of formal classroom contact.

Remember that young people are learning to think critically, and they are searching for inconsistencies in behavior. Talking about obedience in class and later ignoring the speed limit when driving the car is a glaring inconsistency. As teachers, we must seek to model the same quality of life that we would like them to live. This means that if we make a mistake we should admit it and seek to correct the error. Youth don't necessarily expect us to be perfect, but they do expect us to be honest in dealing with our failures and shortcomings. Make a list of the things that might be appropriate for you to do with your class to provide those valuable informal teaching opportunities.

TEACHING ADULTS: It is very important to model ministry

to adults. Christian living is a vital and continuing need. But at some point in the course of spiritual development, adults must become involved in ministry to others. Sitting in class soaking up spiritual nourishment with no outlet for ministry will cause any adult to stagnate. A worthy goal of any teacher is to seek to get all students involved in some sort of ministry. Often this can be as a part of a formal class organization. Visiting those who are sick, following up on visitors, providing hospitality for the families of the ill, and helping those with specific physical and financial needs are just some of the examples of class ministry opportunities.

Another good outlet is for a class to assume the responsibility for a specific ministry project. Perhaps your adult class would agree to be responsible for staffing a children's church program. Some from the class could be responsible for giving general oversight, and others could meet the various staffing and functional needs of that ministry. Look around your church for programs that are lacking adequate leadership and then suggest to your class that they, as a group, minister in one of those programs. Not only will this give your class members an outlet for ministry, but it will set the example for other classes to follow. And in all of this you, the teacher, will be modeling ministry and providing opportunities for the adults you teach to follow your good example.

FOUR

Let Them See
What You're Saying
(On Not Boring Your Students to Death)

Insight on Ministry

A friend of mine once shared an amazing experience with me. It sounds like the kind of story that someone would make up, but my friend Roger personally guaranteed the authenticity of the account.

As the story goes, Roger was working with a man who had a very peculiar habit. Whenever he was talking to a group of people, whether teaching, preaching, or conducting a staff meeting, this man would talk unusually fast. At first Roger thought that perhaps the man was exceedingly nervous, but that didn't seem to be the case. In fact, the man appeared quite composed and relaxed whenever he spoke to a group. Plus this fast talker exhibited no other symptoms of stage fright.

You might not think this so strange because many people talk fast. As a matter of fact, I've worked for years trying to cultivate the practice of speaking more slowly and distinctly — trying to overcome my East Coast heritage. But what puzzled Roger was that this man never talked fast except when he stood up in front of a group.

When my friend could stand it no longer, he finally worked up the courage to ask the gentleman about his quirk. The man explained to Roger that he once had been told that people remember only about 10 percent of what they hear. "Therefore," he reasoned, "why not learn to talk faster? If I say more, then the 10 percent will be more also."

Most of us are acquainted with the line from the poet, "A little learning is a dangerous thing." But few of us know that the next line reads, "Drink deeply or taste not the Pierian Spring." The spring at Pieria, according to Greek mythology, would bestow wisdom and inspiration upon any who might drink from it. Thus the poet's wise exhortation not to dabble in knowledge. Roger's coworker had not drunk deeply from the fount of wisdom. Indeed, he had merely rinsed out his mouth. And so, in his hands, a little knowledge was not merely dangerous, it was lethal.

Actually, the man was on the right track. Although he had misapplied partial knowledge, at least he modified his behavior based on what he knew of how people learn. It's depressing to realize how many people haven't even come that far. Teacher after teacher stands before the class and drones on, oblivious to the fact that students have long since tuned out. A note, written by an eighth-grade student about just such a teacher, was found in the wastebasket of a classroom in Philadelphia. It read: "How can you stay awake? I'm so bored I could lay down on the floor and go to sleep. I don't see how she can talk so much. I wish she would let us talk sometimes."

Countless studies and research projects have taught us much about how people learn. We know, beyond any shadow of doubt, that talking is one of the least interesting and least productive ways of communicating. And yet many teachers wax eloquent, week after tedious week, thinking that they have done their jobs because they have told their students the truth. Consider the following:

- Vision is our dominant sense. More than 80 percent of what we learn is acquired through the sense of sight. Hearing is much lower, with only 10 to 15 percent learned through the auditory channel.

- The average student spends about a third of class time glancing around the room. Why? Because we need adequate visual stimulation on a regular schedule. Unfortunately, many teachers don't take advantage of student desire for visual input.
- All of us can listen far faster than someone can talk — at least four times faster according to researchers. The teacher who only lectures is ignoring students' great mental potential.
- Students need frequent change of pace. An excellent communicator to adults should go no more than five minutes without some variety; average teachers should go less time. And the attention span of youth and children demands even more variation.
- Word meaning can be very confusing. Take the common word *post* as an example. One dictionary gives no fewer than twenty-two distinct definitions. And it doesn't even mention breakfast cereals!
- Personal definition (connotation) of words varies greatly depending on background and experience. What a pastor means when he talks about love may be totally different from what a 1990's single adult understands.
- Vocabulary limitations severely restrict what we can communicate when we limit ourselves to words. Not only do we lack the vocabulary to express precisely what we mean, but students have limited vocabularies too.

I assume that most readers would agree with all the above statements. Many of us probably knew them already. And yet, what are we doing with that knowledge? Walk around some Sunday morning and observe your church's teachers in action. What will many of them be doing? Talking and talking and more talking! Some of them will be standing behind a lectern, clutching the edges with white knuckles. Others may be seated, facing the students or sitting in a circle with them. You may even find some teachers sitting on a desk or others pacing back and forth in front of the class. One thing is certain, most of them will be talking. Or as one Christian educator described it, they will be acting like "Sunday School quarterlies wired for sound."

And what will the students be doing? Attentively hanging on every word? Probably not! More likely they will be talking among themselves or clowning around. Some may be whispering to friends, while others will be writing "surreptitious" notes. The more courteous ones will be daydreaming quietly, at least giving the illusion that they are listening.

It doesn't have to be that way. Lest you think me a total cynic, I know that it's not that way in every case. Indeed, some classes will demonstrate a high level of enthusiasm and vitality. In some classes, significant learning will be taking place — learning that is active, dynamic, life-transforming. But in these classes the teacher will be doing something more than lecturing.

That's the way it can be in your class. You can teach in such a way that students will enjoy learning. They will look forward to Sunday School each week. No, don't stop talking. Verbal communication is valuable — and effective. But it becomes many times more productive when the visual dimension is added to your communication. Perhaps you already use some visual methods. Why not add more? You will observe the impact on your teaching.

The following dozen ideas are just a starting point. Why not try implementing one of them each week? In the course of one quarter of teaching, you will add a significant level of interest and variety to your instruction.

CHALKBOARD. You should be able to find ways to use the chalkboard in practically every lesson. Thought-provoking questions, outlines, diagrams, charts, illustrations, memory verses, and countless other applications are appropriate.

FLIPCHART. This can be used in lieu of a chalkboard or to write information ahead of time that you may want to refer to later in the class. Flipcharts are easier to use if you have an easel to hold them.

MAPS. While you may not need a map every week, they are invaluable for teaching Bible passages that include geography. Imagine how hard it would be for students to visualize Paul's missionary journeys or the route of the Exodus without large, colorful maps of the Middle East.

OVERHEAD PROJECTOR. The overhead projector offers all the benefits of a chalkboard, plus it allows you to prepare transparencies in advance. Some teachers hold student interest by spontaneously drawing transparencies as they teach; others prefer a combination transparency—partially prepared ahead of time and then completed in class. A special benefit of overhead projection is that you can project on as large a screen as needed for all in the class to see easily.

BULLETIN BOARDS. Many teachers prepare bulletin boards to add visual appeal to the room and to reinforce instruction. Both seasonal and topical bulletin boards improve the quality of teaching. Two warnings are in order. First, change bulletin boards regularly so that you maintain interest and attention. Second, plan them so that they don't become just a cluttered collection place where people leave outdated information.

PICTURES. Since all students have trouble visualizing life in Bible times, pictures help them make the transition. Pictures also help students to grasp how Bible truths apply to life today.

CARTOONS. Many teachers find that both newspaper comics and cartoon books provide good material for illustration. Cartoons are especially attention-grabbing when used to introduce lessons. Many teachers have taught themselves to draw simple cartoons and use that skill effectively in teaching. Your local art or graphics supply store sells easy-to-follow guides that can help you learn the skill.

MODELS. Three-dimensional models help teach Bible facts as well as the application of biblical principles. Models of the tabernacle or of Bible-time houses can help students understand hard-to-picture concepts. Models of artifacts like the Dead Sea Scrolls, lamps, chariots, weapons, and musical instruments all add life and vitality to teaching. And if the class together can build the model it's even more valuable.

OBJECT LESSONS. Tangible objects help teach spiritual truths by analogy. For instance, the recipient of a love letter cherishes and reads it carefully. We ought to read the Bible with the same attitude, because it is God's letter to us. Students of all ages respond to effective object lessons.

FLANNELGRAPH. Students can visualize Bible stories much more easily when they are told with a reinforcing tool such as a flannelgraph. Younger children also enjoy manipulating the characters and retelling the story themselves.

PUPPETS. All age groups love puppets. And using them is very easy. One hint is not to have the puppet talk directly to the students, but to whisper things in your ear. Then you can carry on a conversation with the puppet, repeating what the puppet "said to you" for the entire class to hear.

THE TEACHER. The final visual resource that I will mention here is you, the teacher. You are highly visible and teach in many different ways. Your enthusiasm, posture, and facial expressions all contribute to visual teaching. But how you model truth is the most significant way that you teach. Jesus said, "Everyone who is fully trained will be like his teacher" (Luke 6:40, NIV).

Perhaps you are one of the teachers who use visual methods effectively. Congratulations, and keep up the good work. But if you are not using visuals to communicate, why not rethink your approach to teaching?

Studies have shown that when we use visual methods *instead* of talking, students can learn about twice as much in the same amount of time. But when we *combine* visual *with* verbal techniques, students retain up to five times as much as when we just talk. Simply on the basis of economy, as good stewards of the time and skills that God has given us, we should choose the most effective methods available.

Are you using the teaching resource packet that is correlated with your curriculum materials? It offers visual resources to help you teach each lesson more effectively and with higher interest. The suggestions and resources that it offers will help make boredom a thing of the past. For as someone once suggested, it is a sin to bore students to death with poor Bible teaching. Why not resolve today, with God's help, to select one visual method from the preceding list to try each week? Try a visual resource for your next Sunday's lesson. You will find that your teaching will improve dramatically. Both you and your students will be grateful that you did.

Insight from the Word (Part One)

One of the very best ways to stimulate the interest of students (which will help them to learn) is to take advantage of other senses in addition to the sense of hearing, since God has created us as multi-sensory beings. The more of the senses that we employ, the greater the potential for effective teaching.

If employing a variety of senses will contribute to effective teaching, then we ought to observe this principle at work in the teaching ministry of Christ. Since Jesus, the Creator and Sustainer of the universe (John 1:1-3), also understood what those around Him felt and believed (John 2:25), it is logical that He would have taught with visual methods if it were effective. Indeed, such is the case. Jesus' ministry is filled with instances of appealing to a variety of senses.

Utilizing object lessons often is thought of as a contemporary method. But God used objects (stars) to explain His promise to Abraham (Gen. 15:5). Jesus' earthly ministry was filled with the creative use of visual methods as well. Sometimes Jesus used tangible objects as a means to teach a lesson. Read John 6:5-13. In this situation Jesus provided for the needs of the great multitude that was following Him. Why do you think that Jesus asked where the disciples could buy bread to feed the multitude, knowing that there was no place? (vv. 5-6). _____

_____

_____

What was Philip's answer? (v. 7) _____

_____

What did Andrew suggest? (vv. 8-9) _____

_____

What would suggest to you that Andrew was skeptical of the value of the resources that they had? (v. 9) _____

_____

_____

What did Jesus do with the resources that He had available? (vv. 10-13) _____

_____

_____

What was the basic lesson that Jesus taught His disciples, and how did the use of tangible objects communicate and reinforce that lesson? (Compare when Jesus referred back to this event as a reminder of His power, Mark 8:14-21.) _____

_____

_____

_____

_____

Matthew 5–7 is known as the Sermon on the Mount. It is an excellent example of the effective use of visual methods, even though Jesus followed the lecture format. Read Matthew 6:25-34. How did Jesus make use of objects in these verses? _____

_____

How did these objects contribute to the effectiveness of the lesson? _____

_____

What was the lesson that Jesus taught more effectively through the use of visual methods? _____

_____

_____

Scan through chapters 5 to 7. Notice how Jesus' use of highly visual elements in His teaching helped people picture what He was talking about. One caution should be observed in teaching with objects. They never should overshadow the lesson. If the objects employed are so interesting and so captivating that the lesson never is learned, then they are a hindrance rather than a help to good teaching.

Insight from the Word (Part Two)

Obviously, one very important part of teaching is to communicate verbally. There is a certain content that has to be shared with our students. Often the best way to communicate content is verbally. In Titus 2 Paul reminded Titus of the importance of content in teaching. In fact Paul reminded Titus that the needs of certain subgroups within the church were unique and had to be addressed specifically. Paul spoke about the needs of older men (2:2), older women (2:3), young women (2:4-5), young men (2:6), and slaves (2:9-10). And in large part this was to be communicated verbally.

But verbal communication is only part of the task of teaching—even if it is done very effectively and with great creativity. Read Titus 2:7. In addition to talking about what believers should do, how else was Titus to communicate proper behavior?

_____

_____

_____

How would this kind of teaching reinforce what the teacher says? _____

_____

_____

What is the way in which Paul suggested that a teacher can be an example to students? (2:7) _____

_____

In what ways might this be accomplished by a teacher? _____

_____

_____

What three things did Paul suggest that a teacher should "show" in modeling truth (sets an example) in verses 7-8? _

_____

_____

_____

_____

According to verse 8, what will be the results when a teacher models appropriate behavior? _____

_____

_____

Another very important passage that describes the process of modeling behavior is Deuteronomy 6:4-9. In the context, this passage describes what should happen as the Israelites entered the Promised Land. It was imperative, if they wanted to experience God's blessing, to teach the children and all later generations what God had communicated to His people. This meant that effective teaching was important to their prosperity and even to their survival as a nation (Deut. 6:1-3).

Verse 4 is the "Shemah" of Israel — the great affirmation of the unity of the God of Israel. It is a brief summary statement representing the nature of God and His communication. Verses 5 to 9 present the process by which the Word of God was to be taught to all who would grow up in Israel. Read Deuteronomy 6:5-6. What is the starting point for teaching God's Word effectively? _____

_____

How do the ideas that teachers are to totally love God (v. 5) and obey what He has commanded us (v. 6) support the concept of modeling? _____

_____

_____

What happens when a teacher tells students to do (or not do) something, but then contradicts that instruction by his or her own behavior? _____

_____

_____

Can you think of an instance when you or another teacher has contradicted verbal instruction by personal behavior? _____

_____

_____

What was the outcome? _____

_____

_____

Read Deuteronomy 6:7-9 (NIV). Notice that there are three different approaches to teaching suggested in these verses. There is verbal instruction (v. 7), demonstration by the teacher (v. 8), and creation of a general atmosphere where the teaching is done (v. 9). When is it appropriate to talk about God's Law? (v. 7) _____

_____

How would this principle apply to Sunday School teaching?

_____

_____

According to verse 8, God's Word should affect both actions ("tie them . . . on your hands") and thoughts ("bind them on your foreheads"). How can teachers follow these guidelines?

_____

What kind of an influence do you think such behavior would have on your students? _____

_____

_____

Verse 9 suggests that as soon as a person walks into your yard or house, the truth of God should be evident. How would this apply in your classroom? _____

_____

What things contribute to the atmosphere of your classroom?

_____

_____

How can you utilize these to influence your students to under-stand and apply the truth of God's Word? _____

_____

_____

Insight on Teaching

TEACHING CHILDREN: It's obvious to all who have any contact with children that their vocabularies are limited. Be-cause of this most teachers work fairly hard at incorporating a variety of effective nonverbal communication methods. But there is a caution to all children's teachers. Children are ex-tremely literal in their understanding. Abstract object lessons will do more to confuse than to clarify. Figurative language is not meaningful to preschoolers or to many early elementary age children. Objects should be literal (and durable). Pictures, flannelgraphs, and three-dimensional visuals need to be realistic and understandable.

The attitude of the teacher and the atmosphere of the room are powerful influences in teaching children. Teachers need to make the room a pleasant, cheerful place to be. It is very impor-tant that teachers project a loving, acceptant attitude toward all children. Since children's verbal skills are not yet developed, they rely heavily on nonverbal cues to recognize they are wel-come in the class and loved by the teacher.

TEACHING YOUTH: Youth generally have a good compre-hension vocabulary (though they rarely use it when speaking), but again we must be careful not to rely on words alone. They are accustomed to high-interest communication and have relatively short attention spans. Variety and interest are key ideas in communicating with them. Life illustrations are extremely important in helping them bridge the gap between abstract concepts and everyday life.

The role of the teacher in modeling is very important to youth. They are looking for reality in life. Youth also are extremely critical and often intolerant of inconsistencies. When we say one thing and do another we deny the very lessons that we want to teach. When we teachers are living, breathing object lessons, the concepts that we teach are incarnated—made alive in the flesh. This is one of the most effective ways to teach.

TEACHING ADULTS: The most common error I observe among adult teachers is failing to use creative variety in teaching older learners. We often assume that they use and understand words so well that we can rely on words alone. Jesus used objects, illustrations from everyday life, and many interesting stories (parables) to teach adults. And if He, the Master Teacher took such an approach, how much more should we!

Just as with children and youth, teachers need to spend time relating personally to adult students. The teacher's example and offer of personal guidance are important factors in ministering to adults. Of course this means a significant time commitment outside of class. But such a commitment will lead to opportunities for informal contacts that result in growth and maturity.

FIVE

Sunday School Scenarios
(Repairing the Roof Before it Starts Raining)

Insight on Ministry

There is an alleged Chinese proverb that addresses the problem of foreseeing coming circumstances: *It is very difficult to prophesy, especially in regard to the future.*

Yet we must ask ourselves, "What is the future of the Sunday School?" It's a valid question, and we need to answer it as we consider the role of key educational programs in helping to cultivate dynamic, growing churches.

All of us who are committed to high quality Bible education recognize the significant impact the Sunday School movement has had upon the growth of Christianity. Sunday School has been called "The University of the People," and "the most significant lay ministry in the entire history of Christianity." Indeed, many of us can testify to the vital role Sunday School instruction and relationships have played in our own spiritual pilgrimage. This in spite of the fact that most of us can also recount administrative and instructional weaknesses in the Sunday Schools we experienced. (In fact, most Christian educators can cite counter-productive policies and errors in educational judgment that have defamed the terms "Sunday School" and "Christian education.")

This brings us back to the original question. What is the future of the Sunday School? It probably will have more than one future. That is to say the Sunday School of the future will probably take several different forms. And in a large measure, it's up to us to determine what we would like its future to be.

In considering the options, let's borrow a strategy from the futurist. Rather than try to predict the future, let's consider three different scenarios. We'll probably see all three types of Sunday Schools in the future. But one of these likely may become the dominant variety. We must decide which we would prefer and then work toward cultivating that type. The designations that I've chosen for these scenarios are the *Habitual* Sunday School, the *Innovative* Sunday School, and the *Dynamic* Sunday School. Let's consider the characteristics of each type.

The Habitual Sunday School

The Habitual Sunday School is one that blindly repeats what has been done in the past. There seems to be no reason for what is done, other than "we always did it that way." We shouldn't refer to this as the traditional Sunday School. Even though it is highly traditional, it goes beyond tradition in its approach and emphasis. Evaluated tradition can be meaningful, particularly when traditional purpose and vision are retained. Tradition is not automatically bad. It can be a link with the past and provide meaningful continuity with the present and the future.

Leaders of the Habitual type of school place little emphasis on trained teachers. Rather, they accept anyone who comes along. The main goal is to staff the position, with little consideration given to teaching qualifications. As a consequence, those who are serving do so out of duty or obligation. Teaching is viewed as a job that has to be done, rather than a calling from God. It's obvious here that no one evaluates their teaching competency, and no one provides ongoing guidance or training.

69

When leaders deemphasize the importance of teaching and fail to provide training, teachers face constant, often insurmountable, problems with attitude and morale. Such Sunday Schools have very little enthusiasm among either teachers or students. Many classes become little more than babysitting services. Chaos and anarchy often are the rule. What goes on in those classes bears faint resemblance to meaningful Bible study. Since little of value occurs in class, the curriculum is relatively unimportant. No one follows it anyway, so why worry about what materials are used? Consequently, inexpensive materials are preferable to those that are excellent — and often each individual teacher uses whatever he or she wants.

Because of this, Habitual Sunday Schools primarily include children. As they grow older, students tend to drop out so there are few teen classes and rarely any adult classes. Those classes that do continue often have little correlation with other aspects of the church program. Rather than a Sunday School that is an integral part of a coordinated Christian education program, each class is a stand-alone entity.

When we moved to our present community, we encountered a Habitual Sunday School. Someone suggested that we consider attending a certain church in a neighboring town. The newspaper ad was unclear about that church's Sunday School, so my wife called the church office to find out when the Sunday School met, and if it included all age groups. The receptionist couldn't answer our questions, so she called one of the pastors to the phone. He wasn't sure if they even had a Sunday School. He knew they used to have one, but he wasn't sure what ages had been included. The incredible thing was that no one there could answer our question. Since then, we've discovered that this church does have a Sunday School program, but it is a classic example of the Habitual Sunday School, and few people (pastors included, apparently) even care it if exists.

The Innovative Sunday School

Vastly different from the Habitual approach is the Innovative Sunday School. The contrast between the two is great. Innovative Sunday Schools demonstrate flexibility, a high level of enthusiasm, and regular (perhaps even constant) change. Observers sometimes get the impression that innovation and change are the main goals for the program. In the Habitual approach there is a steadfast desire to resist change; however, Innovative leaders seem to seek change compulsively. Often it doesn't matter if the change is for the better or not. What really seems to matter is that there's variety and innovation . . . even if no one knows why.

In order to spearhead such innovation, usually there is a dynamic leader. Such a person often is self-motivated and intensely goal-oriented. This leader's drive, and perhaps power to convince others, is the moving force for innovation. Many of those who follow may do so out of respect, or because of the excitement generated by this leader — or in some cases, even out of awe and intimidation. Naturally, such a program will rise and fall on the skill and personal power of this leader. But if the leader happens to leave the scene, the Innovative Sunday School may well disband or languish until another visionary emerges.

The lack of continuity and absence of ties with the past can create great difficulty for the Innovative Sunday School. The attitude that new is good and dramatic is better can create a "Disneyland mentality." "Last year we re-enacted the flood . . . The year before we crossed the Red Sea . . . How are we going to beat that this year?" Rather than promoting education, these leaders may be more concerned with designing a spectacular extravaganza. Naturally, such unique programs must be tailor-made. Unfortunately, there may be little indication that substantial, long-term benefits will result.

Often the curriculum is "home grown." It is interesting to examine the "self-written" curriculum of some Innovative programs. Curriculum materials may bear marked similarity to published materials, sometimes even having similar titles, outlines, illustrations, and other ideas provided by various independent or denominational publishers. Sometimes the resources for teachers are quite sparse, focusing more on the innovative aspects than on meaningful Bible study.

Some innovation and change are desirable, but constant change and compulsive innovation may turn into a great liability. The Sunday School's purpose must be more than "to do something different." It is good to have excited students, but that in itself is a superficial goal. In the long run it is likely that innovation for the sake of innovation alone will produce minimal impact in the life and ministry of maturing Christians.

The Dynamic Sunday School

Finally we come to the third possibility for the future, the Dynamic Sunday School. Whereas the Habitual style may emphasize traditional patterns and the Innovative approach dramatic change, the Dynamic Sunday School will set quality instruction as its goal. Leaders will include both tradition and innovation in the program, but tradition will be evaluated and change will be purposeful. Continuity and progress will be more important than sudden, compulsive innovation.

The key to a strong educational program is quality teachers. To have such teachers available, leaders must emphasize training and equipping lay persons for ministry. Well-trained, committed teachers don't occur by accident. The well-staffed Sunday School is led by those who know the value of training and have given it high priority. Training teachers is like repairing a leaking roof. If you wait until it's raining, you're too late. We must prepare teachers ahead of time so they are available when needed. Leaders of Dynamic Sunday Schools recognize this — and their roofs never leak.

The Dynamic Sunday School often will show a regular growth pattern. Teens and adults will participate, as well as children. The Sunday School, an integral part of the total church program, will meet very specific goals as it contributes to the overall emphasis of the church. Their curriculum materials will be carefully chosen to ensure achieving stated goals. Each teacher will not do "that which is right in his own eyes" but will recognize that every class contributes to the total program. Direction and progress will be evident as children and youth move through various classes. Adult classes will exhibit a spirit of community as members participate enthusiastically. Excited students will understand and apply Bible truth as they grow toward maturity in Christ.

The results of the Dynamic Sunday School extend far beyond the actual years that students spend there. As children, youth, and adults participate in meaningful Bible study, they come to recognize its relevance for their lives. Regular study of God's Word, with personal application, produces continued growth and maturity. Such refreshing vitality will extend to the total ministry of a church with a Dynamic educational style. Christians who grow through the ministry of a Dynamic Sunday School become excited about ministering to others. Consequently they prepare themselves to teach and to serve in other ways. And those skills inevitably contribute to the entire church, not just to the Sunday School program.

The Sunday School of "Your" Future

You are probably aware that all three types of Sunday Schools exist today, perhaps even in your own community. Yet the long-term impact — the real future of the Sunday School movement — depends on which one predominates. Habitual Sunday Schools will have little long-term impact in creating vital church ministries. In fact, they may be more negative than positive. Many students are "turned off" to Bible study through the Habitual approach.

While Innovative schools are better, their zeal tends to ebb and flow. Innovation is difficult to maintain, and those who provide the drive and direction may be unpredictable. Conducting a Sunday School that's characterized by compulsive novelty or constant variety can become tiring. Motivation may wane and the very innovation that was sought may become a new "tradition" — thus a new Habitual Sunday School evolves.

However, the Dynamic Sunday School has great potential for long-term, increasing impact. It's a place where students develop Bible study skills; they're taught by concerned, well-prepared teachers who love them; and they learn in such a way that God's Word guides and directs their lives.

Obviously a full discussion of how to plan and conduct a Dynamic Sunday School is impossible here. However, the following study should help to give you a better understanding of the biblical goals for effective Christian education. Then there are other resources that can help you and your other leaders to build a Dynamic Sunday School.

Remember, we are the ones who will construct the Sunday Schools of the future. What kind would we like? Let's start building that kind right now. Let's not wait until it starts raining to worry about repairing the roof. If we act now we'll have both excellent Sunday Schools and dry heads too.

Insight from the Word

There is no more important task for a teacher than to understand why teaching is so critical to the life and development of a healthy local church. But this understanding must be based on God's plan for the church universal. If we can understand how God intended the teaching ministry to function, then we can recognize its significance in the life of a growing, dynamic church.

Recently I was visiting a local church and noticed their weekly bulletin. On the program the entire church staff was listed by name and position. This included everyone from the various pastors to the organist. But there was an additional listing. "Ministers" was listed followed by the statement "All church members." This group had come to recognize the biblical truth that every Christian is called to minister and to build up the church — the body of Christ.

Ephesians 4:11-16 teaches this very clearly. Read Ephesians 4:1-16, noting the following divisions. The first six verses of chapter 4 explain all the things that we believers have in common. But then Paul, guided by the Holy Spirit, proceeded to describe the unique functions that we each have as individual Christians. Verses 7-10 explain that each believer has been given special skills (some translations call these gifts of grace) for ministry. "But to each one of us grace [or gifts of grace] has been given as Christ apportioned it" (Eph. 4:7, NIV).

74

Verses 11-16 describe the functioning of these special gifts. There are two kinds of gifts described in these verses. There are leadership gifts (v. 11) and, for lack of a better term, let's call them "followership" gifts (vv. 12-16). The leadership gifts are apostle, prophet, evangelist, pastor and teacher (actually pastor/teacher). The first two (apostle, prophet) were *foundational* gifts (Eph. 2:20), with the second group (evangelist, pastor/teacher) serving as *continuing* gifts. Not everyone receives the continuing leadership gifts. But those who do receive them, are to help the rest of the church in developing their gifts of ministry.

Some translators separate pastor and teacher into two separate gifts, but the punctuation in the NIV accurately reflects what Paul wrote. The commas following "apostles," "prophets," and "evangelists" indicate that "pastors" and "teachers" should be viewed as a unit. In what sense do teaching and pastoring (guiding or counseling) fit together? _____

_____

_____

How might counseling opportunities or the possibility of guiding students grow out of a teaching ministry? _____

_____

_____

Cite examples of when you (or another whom you know) were able to give personal guidance to a student in applying what was taught in a classroom. _____

_____

_____

_____

75

Let's consider how the gifts of ministry ("followership") should contribute to the church by looking at verses 12-16. These verses describe three aspects of our ministry gifts—*purpose* (v. 12), *goal* (v. 13), and *result* (vv. 14-16).

PURPOSE: What is the two-fold purpose of preparing God's people? (v. 12) _____

_____

_____

_____

How does this contradict the idea that only paid staff are to do the work of the church, while the average Christians sit around and watch the professionals? _____

_____

_____

_____

Why is it important that God's people be prepared for works of service? (v. 12) _____

_____

_____

GOAL: The goal of preparing God's people is threefold. We are to reach (1) unity in the faith and in the knowledge of the Son of God. (2) maturity, and (3) attain the fullness of Christ (v. 13). How does the first part of this goal relate to the content of what we teach? _____

_____

_____

_____

Why do you think so many people are ignorant of the content of our faith and know so little about Jesus Christ? _____

_____

_____

According to Bible scholars the second part of the goal (maturity) comes when two conditions are met. Maturity comes when (1) Christian living is practiced consistently and (2) over an extended period of time. How does the ministry of teaching (including the guiding/counseling aspect) contribute to helping a believer to maturity? _____

_____

_____

When a Christian is not mature though professing to be a follower of Christ for many years, what might we conclude is wrong? _____

_____

_____

What would you prescribe as a remedy for such a person? __

_____

_____

RESULT: The result has a twofold dimension (vv. 14-16). One part is negative, the other part positive. What should not be characteristic of believers where the people of God are ministering properly? (v. 14) _____

_____

_____

What qualities characterize spiritual infants? _____

_____

_____

How might these truths explain the susceptibility of some Christians to false teaching? _____

_____

_____

_____

By way of contrast, what positive qualities should be seen in the lives of maturing Christians? (v. 15) _____

_____

_____

_____

From what source should Christians receive their direction in life? (v. 15) _____

_____

How is the picture of a healthy body an excellent metaphor to explain how a church (the body of Christ) ought to function?

(v. 16) _____

_____

_____

_____

What is the end result when those with leadership gifts are equipping the people of God who, in turn, are doing the work of service? (v. 16) _____

_____

_____

Insight on Teaching

TEACHING CHILDREN: Modeling is an excellent way to help children begin to see that all believers should be involved in ministry. We *show* children what is important much more effectively than we can *tell* them. In the very youngest classes, we should model both men and women teaching and working with children. This means including men even in the nursery, or at the very latest in the toddler departments. (I have found that men tend to be more comfortable working with very young children when paired with their wives.) By encouraging men to minister at these ages we help to contradict the all-too-common impression that only women are the teachers.

This practice should continue beyond the younger ages. Children in the Primary and Junior departments need male teachers too. I know of no better way to model a healthy Christian home than to have a husband and wife team-teaching in Sunday School. This not only sets a good example for the children while providing a balanced ministry, but it also can build family unity and joint ministry. In our church we have separate classes for boys and girls in the Junior department. For some time my wife Elaine taught the sixth-grade girls while I taught the sixth-grade boys. We each had our own ministry, but also shared together as we ministered.

TEACHING YOUTH: Team teaching doesn't have to end with the children. Indeed, it is very wise to have husband/wife teams working with youth. I recall an incident when Elaine and I were teaching a high school Sunday School class. We were discussing God's pattern for the family, particularly the husband's responsibility to set the direction for the household. One of the girls piped up, "Oh yeah? Who's the head of *your* house?" As I took a deep breath, Elaine quietly interjected, "My husband is, and let me tell you why I'm so happy that he is." Nothing I could have said ever would have had the impact of that quiet answer to a very significant question.

We also need to encourage our teens to get involved in ministry themselves. All children's classes need helpers with the many activities important to effective teaching. Although we wouldn't want teens missing their own classes regularly, they can minister on a rotation basis. Week-day ministries, youth clubs, children's church, vacation Bible school, and countless other opportunities exist for teens to minister to children. I even have seen older teens assume full teaching responsibility for a class, although that should not be the norm. Getting youth involved in ministry will help us to avoid the "teen exodus" by expecting them to be on the giving and not always on the receiving end of service.

TEACHING ADULTS: If we have been teaching our children and youth, both by precept and by example, that all believers have been given gifts of ministry, then it will be a very simple task to continue the emphasis with adults. Obviously adult classes need to study Bible passages that explain the nature of ministry. These passages, such as Ephesians 4:1-16 should be preached from the pulpit and studied in Sunday School. Both instruction and illustrations should reinforce this basic Bible theme.

But beyond just talking about it, classes can mobilize adults to ministry. Obviously class members need to develop a genuine concern and care for each other. Needs of individuals and families in the class should be prayed for and met by other class members. This could include both financial and personal help. Members of the family of God should support one another.

In addition to ministering to each other, classes can adopt particular ministry projects. For example, an adult class could assume responsibility for staffing a particular children's program. This not only gets adults involved and provides quality ministry, but it prevents the class from being so inwardly focused and preoccupied with its own needs and interests. One church had a great need for children's church leaders. An adult group in the church was concerned about the lack and decided to do something about it. Two couples in the group agreed to assume responsibility for running the program while the rest of the class committed to help the two couples through prayer. Group members also agreed to work in the program themselves and to recruit others to work with the children.

When individual Christians are involved in ministry, and when they are modeling proper involvement, the church will become what it ought to be — a vital healthy body that is growing, maturing, and helping younger Christians to discover and to develop their gifts of ministry.

SIX

Confronting
Worker Burnout
(Burning the Candle at Just One End)

Insight on Ministry

The town where I live is blessed with an overabundance of hardware stores, probably reflecting the "do-it-yourself" passion of many homeowners. We are the ones who prefer the satisfaction (and economy) of accomplishing a task ourselves, instead of calling in a tradesman to work for us.

But the decision to "do it myself" can produce quite interesting situations. Some of us have gotten involved in projects that are way over our heads. We may know what should be done, but things just don't seem to work out right. No matter what we try, certain parts don't fit. What should slip apart easily doesn't budge. Sometimes we need a specialized tool to finish a job, and a "simple task" becomes virtually impossible without it.

At a time like this, a skilled counselor is invaluable. Wise amateur craftsmen learn this lesson early. And so we shop in those stores where such help is available. When my friends and I compare notes, we discover that there is one particular store in town where we all go for help. When amateurs need help we regularly consider Hawthorne Hardware. It's not the largest hardware store in town. It doesn't have the most complete inventory, and I suspect it is not the least expensive. But it does have a knowledgeable, helpful, and gracious staff. No question is stupid, no problem insignificant, and no salesperson too busy to talk through a project with a customer. Because of this, people go out of their way to shop at Hawthorne Hardware.

We usually relate do-it-yourself projects to the home, but the concept applies elsewhere too. There is no place where the do-it-yourself philosophy is more appropriate than in the local church. The measure of true success for a given church is not how many attend the worship service, the size of the missions budget, or even how many attend prayer meeting. A church's success should be defined by the extent to which individual Christians are involved in ministry to each other. The church truly is a do-it-yourself project.

It is unfortunate that many Christians, pastoral staff members included, seem to have forgotten this essential truth. As I visit churches around the world, the number-one problem, by a landslide, is securing adequate staff. Many laypersons seem to have the idea that their duty is to hire pastors who will do the work of the ministry. But this is not what God intended. Church members with leadership gifts should be the guides and resource persons who help other Christians in the body discover and develop whatever special abilities God has given them (Eph. 4:11-16). And every Christian has received special abilities for ministry.

Where Christians are not discovering and developing their ministry gifts, church leaders struggle to find teachers and other workers. This leads to overload for those who are working. These men and women are afflicted with Busy-Person Syndrome, victims of the motto, "If you want to get something done, give it to a busy person." In the church we seem to do this with a vengeance. Consequently, while the many who are observing complain, the few doing all the work become exhausted. And overextended, exhausted workers are prime candidates for burnout.

But we dare not permit this to happen. We must protect those who are most vulnerable. If we allow a worker to experience burnout, both that person and the whole church will suffer. While overwork is a key factor in burnout, it is not the only one. If church leaders become aware of contributing factors, they are more likely to help workers maintain profitable ministry. In his very helpful book *Burnout* (Victor Books, 1987), Myron Rush lists ten factors that cause burnout. Let's see how each of these relates to local church ministry.

Factors Contributing to Burnout

Feeling driven instead of called. One common motivation for church workers is guilt. Sometimes leaders even appeal to guilt as a recruiting device. "If you really love the Lord, you'll certainly be willing to teach this class," or, "If you say, 'no,' how will you answer God in the Day of Judgment?" In other cases, workers may be driven by personal goals such as recognition, proving themselves, or "straightening somebody out." Under these circumstances, the valid goal of ministering to the glory of God may be totally eclipsed.

Failing to pace ourselves. We often forget that maturity develops gradually, rarely as quickly as we might like. A Sunday School teacher who accepts a problem class and plunges in with great vigor, expecting instant transformation, soon will become discouraged. We should approach the tasks of ministering in the same way that we would eat an elephant—one bite at a time!

Trying to do it all ourselves. "Many hands make light work" applies to church work just as well as it applies to moving a piano. Several times Paul used the analogy of a body to describe the church (Rom. 12:4-8; 1 Cor. 12:12-27; Eph. 4:16). A body can be healthy only when every individual part contributes its appointed function. If a few people are doing all the work in a given church, soon no one will be working. Only as each person serves appropriately will that ministry remain strong and vital.

Excessive contact with people's problems. This relates directly to factor number three. When a few are doing all of the work, the emotional drain is incredible. The warning of Jethro, Moses' father-in-law, applies today just as in Moses' day. "You will surely wear out, both yourself and these people who are with you, for the task is too heavy for you; you cannot do it alone" (Ex. 18:18). The solution then was to spread the responsibility; it is the same today.

Majoring on the minors. It is easy to get caught up in details and forget the larger picture. The worker who fails to delegate to others soon will drown in a sea of detail. As you encourage people to assume responsibility for some specific task, other good things happen too. These workers usually develop a greater sense of accountability knowing that they are trusted. And they quickly develop ministry skills that enhance the entire church.

Unrealistic expectations. We must strive and look for realistic growth. People periodically come to me at work complaining of problems with our company. Often their perceptions are correct. But rather than becoming discouraged with our weaknesses, I ask them to think back to where we were earlier. If we see improvement, then we can be encouraged to keep on working. We should expect progress, not perfection.

Developing too many routines. This dilemma often occurs when one church tries to imitate the organizational structure of another (usually larger) church. I once served in a very small church with a Sunday School enrollment of about forty. Had we staffed every department as the denomination recommended, our entire membership would have been insufficient to provide secretaries, let alone fill all the other positions. And we would have had no one left to teach or attend class. Organizational routines are like instructions for putting together toys — the simpler the better!

An inappropriate understanding of God's expectations. Some seem to feel as Elijah did after his confrontation with the wicked Queen Jezebel — "I alone am left; and they seek my life, to take it away" (1 Kings 19:14). There are many faithful who maintain commitment to serving God. God will give each one opportunities to serve, and never demand more of anyone than He enables that person to give.

Poor physical condition. Whether it comes from overwork, illness, laziness, lack of discipline, or intentional abuse, the results are the same. When we are physically weak, ministry becomes a chore.

In my years as a Christian college professor, near the end of each semester students often would come to me questioning the goodness, if not the very existence, of God. Usually my first question was, "How much sleep have you been getting?" If the answer was little or none, I prescribed a good night's sleep before we talked further. As you might expect, frequently there was no need to talk after that.

Continuous rejection. All Christian workers face some rejection. But those responsible for recruiting others seem to struggle more than most. Replies such as, "I'm too busy," "I don't know enough," "I've had my turn, let somebody else do it," or "I'll be glad to help, but I don't want to be in charge" are played over and over. Often the recruiter becomes so discouraged that the only two options seem to be to cry or scream!

Solving the Problem of Burnout

The situation is not hopeless; burnout is not inevitable. Consider these strategies to help alleviate problems and produce far more satisfying ministry experiences for all workers.

Develop a church mission statement. This need be only a simple paragraph (several sentences maximum) that explains why the church exists. No organization that does any serious planning would try to function without such a statement.

When church leaders can identify why their church exists, then all program directors can understand which part of the mission their program helps to accomplish. Further, all workers can understand how they contribute to the overall ministry. This gives them a sense of purpose and an awareness of their significant contribution.

Provide leadership training. It is irresponsible to allow people to serve in positions for which they are ill-prepared. Teachers, ushers, deacons, elders, missions committee members, and all other workers need training. There is no excuse; abundant resources are available to help us train workers.

In some cases, a church may offer its own training classes that follow a regular curriculum. Other training could come through sending workers to workshops or conventions. It may include providing printed resources such as books or magazines. There are many excellent training videos available, some at very reasonable cost. But the best training remains personal contact in which a mature, skilled worker guides and encourages a less experienced person.

Develop a church-wide training/recruitment program. Many churches allow each ministry program to recruit in isolation. This means that often one program competes against another. Since God instructed leaders "to prepare God's people for works of service" (Eph. 4:12, NIV), this task is just as important as preaching or teaching the Word. Those churches doing an excellent job of preparing God's people offer comprehensive training/recruitment programs. Consequently, when a worker is needed, there is a trained pool from which to draw. But truly effective staffing occurs only when pastoral staff members play a key role in supervising both training and recruitment.

Set a policy of limited involvement. It is easy to abuse some of our best workers because they are so willing to serve. This often occurs through encouraging (or allowing) a person to become over-involved.

In one of the churches where I served, one of our best workers was leading five major ministries. As Minister of Education, I was responsible to help correct this abuse. Over a period of months we recruited and trained others to assume four of the five positions. A few months later this worker's spouse expressed thanks to me for giving this person back to home and family.

From that time on, we were careful to limit the number of jobs that one person could hold. The results were happier workers, more effective ministries, and more careful evaluation of program offerings.

Plan regular inspirational/motivational meetings. Even the best workers run out of steam. While no one needs more meetings just for something to do, we do need to provide encouragement for workers. Annual appreciation banquets, worker dedication services, monthly workers' meetings, annual retreats, and inservice training are all ideas that I have tried successfully. We need to let our workers know that they are a valuable and appreciated part of the ministry. And we should be sure to take advantage of local Christian education seminars and conventions. The encouragement and motivation will help to keep workers going.

In business as well as in church life, we admire and praise those people who work with dedication and singleness of purpose. It would be easy to admire the church workaholic, but this is a poor model to hold up for others to imitate. Such a person violates many principles of good leadership and may be doing the very things that ultimately will contribute to burnout. We must carefully review both ourselves and those whom we lead, making sure to discourage unproductive behavior while encouraging excellence in ministry.

Insight from the Word (Part One)

Moses is a classic example of an "accident" who was looking for a place to happen. He possessed a keen sense of mission and felt that he had to be faithful to his calling. Although such motivation is excellent, he had not developed a system to involve others in carrying out that responsibility. And so Moses was working on the verge of exhaustion, trying to "do it all himself." This is the way things were when Jethro, Moses' father-in-law, came to visit. Read Exodus 18:1-12 to understand the setting of Jethro's visit. Then read Exodus 18:13-20. What happened on the second day of Jethro's visit? (v. 13) _____

_____

_____

How do you think the people felt who were waiting for Moses to settle disputes or to solve their problems? _____

_____

_____

How did Jethro respond to what he observed? (v. 14) _____

_____

_____

And what did Moses give as an explanation for what he was
doing? (vv. 15-16) _____

_____

_____

It is of some help to remember that when the Jews left Egypt,
shortly before this time, there were about 600,000 men plus
women and children and others who joined them (Ex. 12:37). A
common estimate is that there were well over 2 million people
in all. And this was the group over which Moses was the sole
judge. The circumstances were complex. Many of these people
had inadequate instruction in the law of God and so needed
special guidance and help in knowing God's will. The situation
was further complicated by the rigors of life in a nomadic setting
where many problems arose out of situations that otherwise
would have been handled routinely. What was Jethro's conclu-
sion after hearing Moses' explanation of his procedures? (v. 17)

_____

_____

What were the two consequences of Moses' procedures that
Jethro suggested would happen? (v. 18) _____

_____

_____

_____

And what did Jethro suggest doing about the problem? (v. 20)

_____

_____

_____

Jethro's plan included three distinct elements. Read Exodus 18:21-27. What was the first element of Jethro's suggestion to Moses? (v. 21a) _____

_____

_____

_____

What task of ministry in the local church today would parallel this function? _____

_____

_____

What was the second element in the strategy that Jethro suggested? (v. 21b) _____

_____

_____

Although it is not specifically stated in the text, what help do you think that Moses provided for those whom he chose? __

_____

_____

What was the third element in the strategy that Jethro proposed? (v. 22) _____

_____

_____

How would this have greatly reduced the load that Moses had
been carrying? _____

_____

_____

What were the two consequences of the strategy that Moses'
father-in-law proposed to Moses? (v. 23) _____

_____

_____

_____

What is a clue in Exodus 18:23 that Jethro's advice came from
God, even though God did not speak directly to Moses as He
had earlier? (Ex. 3:4ff) _____

_____

_____

Insight from the Word (Part Two)

A common illustration of the proper functioning of the body of
Christ is the analogy of a human body. There are three major
passages that describe the church in this manner. These are
Romans 12, 1 Corinthians 12, and Ephesians 4. Read 1 Corinthians 12:12-26. How do verses 12-13 clearly reinforce the con-

cept that every believer is important to the body of Christ, regardless of social position or nationality? _____

_____

_____

_____

What kind of a human body would we have if the conditions stated in verses 14-17 existed? _____

_____

_____

_____

How would a church emphasizing only one "gift" be similar to a grotesque human body that consisted of only an eye or only an ear? _____

_____

_____

_____

In contrast to a malformed, dysfunctional entity, in what way has the church been equipped to function? (vv. 18-20) _____

_____

_____

_____

How does a proper understanding of the body of Christ overcome feelings both of superiority and also of inferiority? _____

_____

_____

_____

The body analogy contrasts the highly visible parts (those that we give great attention) with the truly important parts (the fragile parts that are hidden inside) which are critical to a healthy body (vv. 21-24a). In the church, leadership gifts are highly visible; but less visible gifts that function behind the scenes are vitally important. List some of these leadership gifts.

_____

_____

What are some of the less visible, but critical ministries that contribute to the life and vitality of a healthy church? _____

_____

_____

_____

How do verses 24b-26 reinforce the concept that everyone's contribution is vital if a church is to be strong and healthy?

_____

_____

_____

_____

Insight on Teaching

TEACHING CHILDREN, YOUTH, AND ADULTS: Regard-less of which age group we teach, there are certain basic con-cepts that we must remember. The following suggestions follow the guidelines for avoiding worker burnout. Ideally many of these services should be provided by leaders in a church. But if they are not offered, you can protect yourself by following these simple suggestions.

1. Learn how your ministry fits in with the overall mission of your church. If your church has a clearly stated mission it should be easy. If not, find out from your pastor or other key leaders why your church exists. Then find out what the particular ministry in which you are serving contributes to accomplishing that pur-pose. Write out a simple statement of how your ministry activi-ties fit in with those purposes.

2. Ask for training in how to do your job better. Many curricu-lum publishers offer resources to help those using the materials. They may even send people to help to train the teachers. At-tend local Christian education conventions or seminars. Sub-scribe to a Christian education magazine and read books about your type of ministry.

3. Develop a teacher recruitment/training program. Although ev-ery church should have an on-going recruitment/training pro-gram, you can develop your own if one is lacking. Recruit a worker to assist with your ministry. Help this assistant to under-stand how you prepare and teach, and gradually give this person increased responsibility. Such in-service training is crucial to any effective training program. When your assistant is prepared, en-courage that person to teach another class and to recruit an assistant even as you find another assistant.

4. Follow a policy of limited involvement. You cannot do every-thing. When you do try, you usually wind up doing nothing well. And you burn out in the process. Rather than try to do every-thing, it is far wiser to develop other teachers (suggestion #3) who can continue to minister in needed areas. Learn how to say no and don't bear the guilt of those who should be involved in ministry but are avoiding responsibility. Recently I saw a poster which read, "I'm sorry, but lack of planning on *your* part does not constitute an emergency on *my* part!" We could paraphrase this, "Lack of serving on another person's part does not constitute guilt on my part!"

5. *Plan regular times of inspiration/motivation.* If your leaders provide such ministry, rejoice and call them blessed. But if not, you can provide inspiration and motivation for yourself. Form a support group of teachers in similar ministries to get together and share ideas with each other. These can be from your own church, or from other churches in the area. Read through and discuss resources on effective teaching. Pray together and then covenant to pray for each other during the week. You might even plan accountability times to check on each other throughout the week to make sure that you are not waiting until the last minute to begin preparation. It also is wise to recruit prayer partners from your congregation who will agree to pray for you on a regular basis. Sometimes such people even will be willing to assist occasionally in your ministry.

Quality ministry by each Christian is vital to the health of the body of Christ. Without it, the church will be weak and ineffective. But when all Christians understand how God has equipped them to serve, and when they use those skills to minister to others, the church will grow and serve to the glory of God.

SEVEN

A Parable
for Spring
(The Gardener and the Garden)

As I sit at my computer writing in January, spring is almost here—it's just around the corner. Even as you read this, some who are more skeptical may think that I'm rushing the season a bit. But I'm right and I can prove it. Many of you could offer the same evidence if you only stopped to think about it.

Perhaps you expect me to say that I just saw the first robin of spring. But often we can see robins from further north, shivering all winter long in our area. And we certainly can't depend on a brief spell of warm weather to signal the advent of spring. Such a false prophet can come at any time, only to be exposed by the renewed fury of Old Man Winter.

But there are other more reliable signs. These signs vary depending on where you live. In the eastern mountains, a brilliant patch of glowing yellow coltsfoot, visible through patches of snow, may be the signal. In the deep south, spring may be heralded by the welcome greening of dry cypress trees. Or perhaps it's the resurrection ferns uncoiling in the live oak trees. And nearly depleted ponds, drying out through the winter, once again will grow, teeming with fresh life.

Farther west, the temperature change may be much less a reliable indicator than in the east. Spring is tied more directly to the coming of the rains than to the temperature. The desert, one day dry and brown, could burst forth the next with life and color. As hillsides pass through various stages in their transition from brown to green, there is no mistaking reality; spring has arrived!

There remains yet another indicator of spring that arrives before any of these, but still is unmistakable in its message. We may be surrounded by the withered remains of last year's vegetation or looking out on shrunken ponds. In the northeast a blizzard may be howling outside. Where I live (near Chicago) there probably is snow on the ground. Into all of this comes the first and the most reliable indicator that winter is not forever and that spring indeed will arrive eventually. The bleakest and most forbidding day of winter is brightened by this herald of spring: The seed catalog has arrived!

Who has not been cheered by the advent of the seed catalog? But its delivery is only the beginning. Following its joyous arrival, the seed catalog offers many hours of thinking, planning, and (if the truth were to be known) hours of dreaming pleasure. Row upon row of lush green plants promising a banquet of fresh nutritious vegetables.

Of course where I live, there are many months between the catalog's arrival and the harvest. For us, the danger of frost isn't past until May 10. And there is lots of work between the seed catalog and the table. Sometimes it seems as though every rabbit, squirrel, raccoon, ground hog, and possum in the vicinity views me as a smorgasbord custodian. Then too, the destruction from one of our son's soccer balls can equal a family of raccoons any day.

But if I make it past the planning and the frost, the planting, the predators, and the soccer balls, my garden still must survive those inevitable dry weeks in the middle of the summer. Mulching helps to conserve vital moisture, but often I need to supplement God's rationing in July and August. As I walk to the back of our lot I gaze with concern on our garden, lovingly planned and tended (by Elaine as well as by me) but now struggling for survival. Survival is spelled w-a-t-e-r, just yards away flowing from the faucet at the back of our house. What I need is an adequate delivery system. This is the time when a garden hose becomes man's best friend. It solves the problem of how to provide water in sufficient quantities to supply the needs of a dehydrating garden. Now hear the Parable of the Gardener.

A Parable

And it came to pass that early in the summer, a homeowner was about to leave on a journey. And he called unto himself a gardener, and he said to that gardener, "I am about to leave on a journey. See this garden, yea verily the garden that I love? Care for this garden that I love, and when I return, I will give unto you that which you have earned."

And so the owner left for his journey, and the gardener did unto the garden that which was needed. And it came to pass in the seventh month of the year, that the gardener said to himself, "Surely, are there not still many weeks until cometh the harvest? And yet look at this garden. Of a truth it is dry unto destruction and lacks that which is needed, even water. Shall I now forsake that which has been entrusted to me, even this garden which brings the owner much pleasure? Shall I abandon it utterly? No, I will get myself up to his house which is nearby, and I will provide that which is most needed for his garden."

And so the gardener got himself up to the house, even the owner's house as he had said. And that gardener took one hose which he attached to one faucet at the back of the house, and began to supply water which was greatly needed for the garden that the owner loved. Notwithstanding, there were yet four other faucets at the back of that house, each with its own hose, which he did not use.

And it came to pass that the owner returned from the far country. Then he came to inspect that which brought him much pleasure, even the garden that he loved. And when the gardener had greeted the owner who had returned from the far country he said unto the owner, "Sir, you have come from a far country and the journey has been long. Come now, refresh yourself. Share with me my iced tea, and let us go look at this garden that you have given unto me to tend. Yea, verily, I am weary unto death from providing that water which is needed for your garden."

And the owner looked and saw that the gardener was working hard with one hose providing water for the garden that he loved. But indeed the garden was large, and that which did not receive water was dry and withered, and had grown up in brambles to become the habitation of all sorts of wild creatures and creeping things. Now the owner recalled that there were yet four other hoses near unto four other faucets at the back of the house which belonged to him. And the owner said unto the gardener. "Are there not yet four other hoses near unto the four faucets at the back of the house that belongs unto me? Why then do you not also use these four other hoses and so provide that which is most needed for this garden that I love?"

"Sir, do not be so hard upon me I pray you," replied the gardener. "You know that this one hose is the one that I have used these many years. Say not that I should use the other four hoses. I am much less familiar with those hoses. Would it not take much time to attach these hoses, even the four, to the faucets at the back of your house? And how do I know that they would not leak? Yea, verily after all my labor they might even spray that which is most needed for this garden that you love upon my garment. And then I would have grief upon grief."

And it came to pass that the owner called before him that wicked and unprofitable gardener. And he said unto the gardener, "Did I not say unto you that this garden, even this garden that I love, has brought me great pleasure? And now my soul is deeply grieved when I see that you have forsaken that which is good, to use only the one hose that is convenient to you. Not only shall I not pay you that which you want, but I will hold you accountable for all of the losses that shall come from this garden which you have neglected."

And the owner utterly cast out from before him that unfaithful gardener. And he gave unto another the position that had belonged to the first gardener.

The Interpretation

Now hear the explanation of the parable of the gardener. The garden is those students whom we teach, and the water is the truth that we teach to them. The owner of the garden is God who has given us responsibility to teach the Word to those whom He loves. The gardener is the teacher and the hoses are channels of communication. The familiar hose is lecture and the four other hoses are other channels of communication — sight, touch, taste, and smell. These are the four channels that we most often ignore in teaching.

It's all too easy to see the application of this parable today. Many of us who teach can be accused of behaving just as the unfaithful gardener. I have interviewed countless teachers throughout the United States and Canada. Teachers of children through adults all agree that lecture is far less effective than other teaching methods. And yet, almost without exception, lecture is the dominant method used. Sometimes it even is used to the exclusion of all others.

Even though we know that we can increase effectiveness by adding visual communication to our spoken words (see chapter 4), we still fail to use it as we ought. And if we add other techniques, we multiply our potential for effectiveness many times.

And yet most of us revert to the one hose that is most familiar, frustrated that it supplies only a limited volume of water. Students grow tired of listening, and teachers grow tired of talking. Isn't it about time that we connect the other four hoses and multiply the effectiveness of our teaching? Our students will learn more and a delightful fringe benefit is that this variety will add a new dimension to our excitement as teachers. Let's stop walking into class week after week, cranking out lecture after lecture. Rather, may we seek to guide our students into dynamic, vibrant learning experiences. When we appeal to a variety of senses with our teaching methods, we will approach class with renewed enthusiasm and confidence. And learners will come with keen anticipation ready and willing to learn the Word of God.

Epilogue

And it came to pass on another day that the owner arrived home from a journey into a far country. And he found his garden strong and healthy, tended by a faithful gardener. This good gardener was using all five hoses to provide that which was needed for the garden. And the garden bore fruit, some fortyfold, some sixtyfold, and some a hundredfold. And the own-er called unto him the gardener and said, "Well done, good and faithful servant, enter into the joy of your master."

Insight from the Word (Part One)

In his classic work *Jesus — The Master Teacher* (now long out of print), written in the early twentieth century, Dr. Herman H. Horne called attention to the outstanding teaching techniques of Jesus. His goal was to demonstrate the marvelous diversity and the unquestioned effectiveness of Jesus' teaching. Dr. Horne lamented that "those who are interested in education have not known about Jesus, and those interested in Jesus have not known about education." Fortunately this has been rectified to a large degree with many outstanding educators committed both to Jesus Christ and also to the authority of the Word of God.

Dr. Horne categorized Jesus' methods and then illustrated each of these approaches. He explained how Jesus used prob-lems, conversations, questions, answers, discourses, (lectures), parables, Scripture, special occasions, contrast, concrete illustra-tions (object lessons), symbols, imagery (figures of speech), as well as building on what students already knew. All of these and more contributed to the unprecedented effectiveness of Jesus' teaching ministry. "When Jesus had finished saying these things, the crowds were amazed at His teaching, because He taught as one who had authority, and not as their teachers of the law" (Matt. 7:28-29, NIV).

Jesus was not the only biblical person to use a variety of tech-niques. Many of the Old Testament prophets behaved more like actors putting on a dramatic presentation than teachers lecturing. And yet somehow today many people feel as though they should be able to just talk, use one channel of communication, and teach effectively. The Bible is filled with illustrations of effective, creative teaching methods. Let's consider a few of those who communicated so dramatically at God's direction. Read Jeremiah 13:1-11. What did God tell Jeremiah to do?

_____

_____

What was the purpose of this elaborate visualization? _____

_____

_____

Why did God have Jeremiah go through this process rather than telling the people of Judah what He was going to do? _____

_____

_____

What do you think was the impact of Jeremiah's object lesson?

_____

_____

Read Ezekiel 4:1-3. Summarize what God told Ezekiel to do.

_____

_____

_____

What could Ezekiel have done that would have been a far easier task? _____

_____

_____

_____

Why do you think that God directed Ezekiel to communicate through the model city? _____

_____

_____

How do you think the people responded to the message that Ezekiel communicated? _____

_____

_____

Read Ezekiel 4:4-8. Summarize what God told Ezekiel to do.

_____

_____

_____

How do you think Ezekiel felt about the assignment? _____

_____

_____

_____

How would you have responded to such a teaching assignment?

_____

_____

_____

What conclusions can we draw about the role of creative methods in communicating God's Word? _____

_____

_____

_____

Insight from the Word (Part Two)

Entire books have been devoted to the subject of the teaching style of Jesus. We will consider only a brief sample of the wide diversity. Read Matthew 22:15-22. The Pharisees were rigid in their observance of the religious rituals that they had established. They hated Rome and anyone who supported or even tolerated Roman rule. On the other hand, the Herodians were Jews who had sided with the Roman rule and cooperated with the authorities. Why would two such unlikely groups come to Jesus together? _____

_____

_____

What would have happened if Jesus had said, "Pay taxes"?

_____

_____

And what would have happened if He had said, "Don't pay taxes"? _____

_____

How did the use of creative methods resolve the tension and graphically communicate to those questioning Jesus in this situation? _____

_____

_____

_____

Read Matthew 18:1-9. Why do you think that Jesus' disciples came asking Him the question in verse 1? _____

_____

_____

How did Jesus help the disciples understand His answer by appealing to the sense of sight? _____

_____

_____

List the figures of speech (word pictures) that Jesus used in teaching His disciples about the importance of children in His kingdom. _____

_____

_____

_____

_____

_____

_____

How do you think these illustrations helped the disciples to "see" what He was trying to communicate to them? _____

_____

_____

_____

Based on how God told some of the prophets to communicate and how Jesus communicated to His followers, what principles can we observe that should influence the way we teach our students? _____

_____

_____

_____

_____

If you were to include such principles in your teaching more often, what do you think the result would be? _____

_____

_____

_____

_____

What might prevent some teachers from adopting creative, varied methods in their teaching ministry? _____

_____

_____

What compelling reasons can you think of to convince those volunteers who might resist using creative methods in teaching their students? _____

_____

_____

What could convince you to use more creative and varied methods as you teach? _____

_____

_____

How will your teaching be different because of what you have learned in this session? _____

_____

_____

_____

_____

_____

Insight on Teaching

TEACHING CHILDREN: Most teachers are aware of the need for creativity and varied methods in teaching children. Children have limited verbal skills so generally teachers of children employ alternatives. It is very important to try using some of the varied methods suggested in the curriculum materials you are using. Obviously visual methods are valuable. Pictures, flannel-graphs, videos, and other teaching tools all are helpful to communicate visually.

Teachers of young children should be careful not to use abstract object lessons that may confuse more than clarify. Preschool and early school-age children are very literal in their understanding. I recall using a broken clock as a "very effective" object lesson with junior-age children. The lesson was rather abstract, but I was sure that juniors could handle it. The next week several asked me if I had gotten my clock fixed yet. I began questioning those who asked me, and not one of them could remember why I had showed them the clock. In this case the object had totally overshadowed the lesson, and I had failed to achieve my objective.

When tempted to lecture, try guided conversation as an effective way to keep your finger on the pulse of your students. It keeps the verbal communication from being a monologue and helps the teacher discover how much the children are learning. Besides it is a much more natural mode of communication since this is how we normally communicate with each other.

TEACHING YOUTH: Many teachers struggle with maintaining some semblance of order in youth classes. The teens tend to talk and fool around in an undisciplined manner. However, to me it is even worse to have a class of teens who sit in absolute silence. When they are talking, you at least can get some sense of where their minds are and how they feel. Young people sitting in passive silence are abnormal. A good class is one where there is dialogue, conversation, humor, and a normal give and take. Rather than attempting to lecture, it is far more effective to discuss important concepts with teens. This means asking them questions and then really listening to the answers.

Illustrations that relate to the daily experience of your students are conducive to life-related teaching. Sometimes beginning with a problem that they face and then seeking Bible answers is very effective. In this approach, the entire class works together to solve a genuine problem. Effective resolution comes through teacher and students working together to discover the answers from God's Word. Good curriculum materials will address the significant problems that teens face. But don't feel that you always need to tell students the answers. Even if you know the solution to a given problem, your teaching will be far more effective if you involve class members in seeking biblical answers.

TEACHING ADULTS: Although most adults have developed good verbal skills, lecture still is a weak way to communicate with them. In workshops I often ask participants to rank, according to their effectiveness, a series of methods that commonly are used with adults. Invariably lecture comes in at the bottom of the list. Yet when I ask them to list the order of most common usage, lecture, as noted in chapter 3, is at the other end of the list — the very top.

Rather than relying on lecture alone, we need to supplement it with varied methods, especially those that are visual in nature. The use of flip charts and chalkboards greatly enhances teaching. Brief segments of appropriate video tapes can be very effective. And these needn't necessarily be instructional videos. A drama that portrays a particular situation could be used to introduce a subject. (Make sure to use only the relevant section of the video.) Other visual techniques include object lessons, pictures, figurative language, and picturesque descriptions.

Illustrations that come from the life and experience of your students always will help them envision the truth that you are trying to communicate. And remember, try to appeal to as many senses as possible, in addition to that of hearing.

EIGHT

Beyond Sunday
School Solutions
(When "Jesus" is Not the Answer)

Insight on Ministry

Recently I visited a pastor friend and came away chuckling at one of the funniest stories I'd heard in a long time. A pastoral associate of my friend was conducting the children's sermon — a time in their worship service when the children are invited to the front of the sanctuary for a special message. On this Sunday the pastor had planned to interact with the children through question and answer. He asked the children if they knew what was small with a bushy tail, ran around the lawn, and gathered nuts. A boy in the back of the group spoke up, "I know the answer's Jesus, but it sure sounds like a squirrel to me!" Needless to say, the pastor experienced far more interaction than he had anticipated.

One of the reasons why this anecdote is so funny is that all of us can visualize the young boy. He has come to think that Christian educators only ask simplistic questions. Questions that usually can be answered with "God," "Jesus," or "The Bible."

The kind of answers that my eldest son Mark calls "Sunday School answers."

Mark and I have a running disagreement about that expression. The summer that he turned fifteen, he began working as a junior leader in a Christian Service Brigade camp. As he learned to work with younger boys, he came to recognize the importance of stimulating them to think. This means rejecting superficial answers. And so, the source of our disagreement.

When Mark receives a superficial response he says, "Sunday School answer!" in a disparaging tone of voice. It's a phrase that I dislike very much, because superficial answers are not unique to Sunday School. But from his observation of Sunday School, Mark maintains that many questions and most answers are shallow. To him, all answers that are given without thinking are "Sunday School answers." Especially if "Jesus" is given when the correct answer should be "a squirrel."

But it doesn't have to be that way, does it? Can't we train our teachers (or educate ourselves) to avoid superficiality? If we do teach in a routine or simplistic way, we may be demonstrating a basic weakness in our understanding of our task. In my experience, this understanding usually begins at our desk (or in the living room, or at the kitchen table, or wherever we prepare our lessons). We cannot be skillful teachers if we are incompetent students. Let's look at some suggestions from skillful teachers for effective lesson preparation.

Take Time to Study the Bible

Although it may seem too obvious to mention, often there is a breakdown right at this point. Some teachers look only at the lesson materials. They ignore the Bible. And even those who do study the Bible may not realize what they are trying to accomplish. We must study so that we understand the biblical principle (the Bible truth) in the assigned passage.

The Bible is God's inspired Word. He gave it without error and has preserved it for us so that we can rely upon it without hesitation today. But many people seem to forget that God gave it to reveal Himself and His expectations. He has revealed things to us that we couldn't know any other way. The Bible is not just a collection of good stories. All Bible content is included for a very specific purpose. In John 20:30 God's Spirit revealed through John that Jesus did many other things that were not recorded, and (John 21:25) that innumerable books could not contain all of Christ's unrecorded teachings.

Every word included in Scripture was selected for a very specific reason. Therefore as we study any passage, we need to ask: What is the truth that God is revealing through this passage? This means understanding the facts of the passage, but not stopping there.

For example, read through the account of the Israelites at Jericho (Josh. 6). You may have mastered the historical facts when you can recount the events of the passage. You know that the Israelites marched around the city once each day, and seven times on the seventh day. You even know what happened after the final circuit. But you are not finished studying. It still is a history lesson at this point. You must ask what God desires to teach us from this passage. This lesson is the Bible truth. One Bible truth in this passage (and there always is more than one) is that God blesses complete obedience. This is a principle that applied to the Israelites, and it applies to us today, even though we are not marching around any cities.

We are not ready to teach the Bible until we have studied the passage and understand the spiritual truths that God has revealed. Our task is to go beyond teaching ancient history, even though it is inerrant, inspired history. We also must teach the truths God reveals through those accounts—the principles of the Word. In class we should teach both facts and principles. But we cannot teach them in class until we have understood them in our study. Then we are ready to profit from a second suggestion from well-trained teachers.

Prepare Your Lesson Presentation Backward

Yes, that's right; approach your preparation in reverse. It's too bad publishers can't write all lesson materials this way. But I'm afraid it would cause too much confusion. Scripture Press (and other curriculum publishers) presents the lesson materials as you will teach them. But in your weekly preparation, first you should consider the outcome of the lesson. The outcome is what you want to happen in the lives of your students. How do you want them to respond?

Most publishers list the lesson aims (or objectives) right at the beginning of the lesson. This is so all of your preparation can be directed toward those particular outcomes — the Bible truth(s) that students should know, and the appropriate life response. Each lesson you teach should include a Bible knowledge aim and a life response aim. These describe the knowledge and behavior outcomes that we expect as the result of our teaching time.

Now we are ready to move one step backward to the middle of the lesson. Once we have determined what we want our students to know and do, and have thought of appropriate responses, we are ready to plan how to help our students discover that truth. Your teacher's manual will suggest ways to help learners discover the Bible facts and principles.

Highly effective teaching always includes more than *telling* our students what God has said. Effective teachers employ a wide variety of methods to guide learners into discovering truth for themselves. Naturally, methods must be appropriate to the age group. And they should vary from week to week. Even the best method becomes stale and ineffective when it is used every single week.

By this point in your preparation you have considered how you want your students to respond, and you have planned ways to help them discover God's truth. Now you are ready to take the final step backward to the beginning of the lesson. It is time to plan how to get started — how to focus student attention.

Remember, all of your students arrive with different feelings and expectations. One may come from a family argument in the car on the way to church. Another may be worried about the coming week, or may be feeling guilty about something from the previous week. Some are excited, some expect to be bored, and others still are asleep. It's our job to break into their consciousness and focus each one on the lesson for the day. It probably will not happen by employing the most commonly used lesson introduction, "Please turn in your Bible to. . . ."

Instead we must plan learning activities that will meet each student where he or she is, and bring each to a common place. Then all can discover God's truth together. It seems like an impossible task, but never forget that the Holy Spirit is ministering to you as the teacher and also to each of those learners gathered with you. He will help you use suggestions that are provided in the teacher's manual, as well as others that you may think of. He will help draw your learners away from distractions and focus their attention on those things that God wants them to learn.

Put It All Together

Now that you have worked through your lesson in reverse, think your way through it from the beginning to end. What are you going to do to get the lesson moving? Each student is thinking about his own concerns. The learning activities that you begin with should help them leave those concerns and focus on the lesson at hand. Those activities should be interesting and attractive.

After you have focused their attention, how are you going to guide them into discovering truth from God's Word? These methods should be interesting and varied. They should guide your students into discovering both biblical facts and principles.

Finally, think about the response of your learners. What activities will you employ to help them begin applying what they discovered in class? This application should begin before they leave class. It should continue on through the week and become consistent behavior in their lives.

As you try these suggestions from trained teachers, you ought to see the quality of your teaching improve. But don't stop there. Share what you have learned and tried with other teachers. Appoint yourself as an "ad hoc committee of one" for teacher training. Praise God for the blessings that you will see in your own teaching and in the teaching of your associates. Perhaps we will receive fewer "Sunday School answers." And our students may even recognize the difference between "Jesus" and "a squirrel" too.

Insight from the Word (Part One)

There are many kinds of questions that we can ask our students. Generally speaking, questions of any quality are better than none at all. But to gain the most benefit from the questions that we ask, they should be well-planned and appropriate to the class. This means that we use questions to draw our students into the teaching/learning process. Good questions will help to stimulate thought and promote serious thinking among the students.

If we are good at asking questions, we will encourage students to begin asking questions also. The questions that come from students help us to take their spiritual and intellectual pulse. Student questions help us to look inside those individuals and discover the level of understanding and practice in their lives. Questions from students will encourage others in your class to think more deeply about a given topic and honestly examine their personal beliefs and feelings.

Let's consider some of the questions that Jesus asked and the consequence of those questions. In an earlier lesson we considered how Jesus approached the Samaritan woman at the well of Sychar. Read through the account of Jesus' masterful instruction of the Samaritan woman in John 4:4-42. How did Jesus begin the conversation? (v. 7) _____

_____

_____

Do you think that this was a good way to open the conversation? Why, or why not?

_____

_____

_____

The woman then asked Jesus a question; but rather than answer it, Jesus seemed to take a different approach (v. 10). How did Jesus' answer, trigger another question in the woman's mind? (v. 11) _____

_____

_____

What additional question did she ask Jesus? (v. 12) _____

_____

_____

_____

Why do you think that Jesus did not answer the question about whether or not He was greater than Jacob, but directed the woman's attention to her real need, not just her curiosity about this person talking with her? (vv. 13-14) _____

_____

_____

How did Jesus' communication deal with an area where the woman felt an immediate need, before He attempted to progress toward considering her deeper needs? (v. 15) _____

_____

_____

Once again Jesus did not allow the conversation to focus on the immediate, physical concerns but addressed a deeper spiritual problem (vv. 17-19). At this point in the conversation, Jesus and the woman were communicating about the real spiritual issues of life. And Jesus took the opportunity to continue teaching the woman and others from the region (vv. 21-26, 39-42). How can we utilize Jesus' strategy in teaching people today?

_____

_____

How might it be beneficial when the person being taught is not prepared to plunge into a discussion of spiritual truth? _____

_____

_____

Insight from the Word (Part Two)

Many times Jesus used questions to confront His listeners with truth that they did not want to admit. Read Luke 6:6-11. The Pharisees were opposed to Jesus and were looking for a reason to condemn Him. Among other things, they were trying to catch Him in breaking their interpretation of Sabbath rules so that they could accuse Him of working on the day of rest. How did Jesus' question confront them with a dilemma? (v. 9) _____

_____

_____

Probably the same confrontation in the synagogue is described in Matthew 12:8-14. How did Jesus' second question (Matt. 12:11) further complicate the Pharisees' answer? _____

_____

What do you think would have been the answer of the Pharisees to questions Jesus asked about the value of a person? (v. 12)

_____

_____

Mark's account of the same event (Mark 3:1-6) explains that the Pharisees remained silent and refused to answer Jesus' questions. Why do you think they were not willing to answer the question?

_____

_____

_____

Jesus also used rhetorical questions. These are questions that the teacher really does not intend for the student to answer. They are used to get students thinking. Read Luke 6:39-42. List the rhetorical questions that Jesus asked in teaching this lesson.

_____

_____

_____

Can you recall other times when Jesus chose to use rhetorical questions with His students when teaching? If so, list those that you can recall or discover in the Gospels. _____

_____

_____

_____

Jesus regularly taught in such a way that His students were stimulated to ask questions of Him. One of the most familiar instances of this approach can be found in Matthew 13:1-23. After the Parable of the Sower, what did the disciples ask Jesus? (v. 10) _____

_____

_____

And what was His reply? (vv. 11-15) _____

_____

_____

_____

How did Jesus put His disciples into a different category from those who were hardened and insensitive? (vv. 16-17) _____

_____

_____

And then what did Jesus do to continue His ministry with those disciples who wanted to learn more? (v. 18) _____

_____

_____

Insight on Teaching

Whenever we teach, certain questions are going to be raised in the minds of our students. Generally we can group these questions into three categories. And it helps our teaching if we recognize the questions that students ask in their minds, even if

DEVELOPING THE TEACHER IN YOU

they don't express them. The most basic question is: *Do I under-stand what is being taught?* This question applies to all kinds of lessons in any teaching situation. If a student fails to understand the concepts that are being taught, little more can take place. For this reason, teachers should ask questions that probe the ideas of the lesson. The answers that students give will provide feedback to let us know how we are communicating.

We also should encourage our students to ask us questions when they fail to understand something. Students should under-stand our feeling that the only bad question is the one a student fails to ask. We ought to encourage openness and freedom to question. I once sat in on a very confusing class presentation. Although the teacher was not encouraging questions, the stu-dents were used to having the opportunity to ask them from sitting under other teachers. Part way through the confusion, a student finally said, "What in the world are you saying? I don't have the faintest idea what we are talking about!" The teacher had missed the previous clues that the students were confused, but with that question he finally became aware of the need to clarify his instruction.

A second implicit question in students' minds is: *Do I really believe what is being taught?* This question goes much deeper than just the content. It has to do with the acceptance of the lesson. Many times people hear an instructor and understand every-thing that is said, but somehow disregard it. They may give mental assent to the truth, but really not believe it. This is especially true in spiritual areas, but it also relates to any area where believing something should affect our behavior. A person may "know" that fatty foods are bad for our health, yet still consume large quantities of french fries. Or we may know that it is important to study the Bible, pray, and serve in our local church, but still not do any of those things.

In our churches we rarely encourage people to question spiri-tual assumptions. And so, we don't confront them with the need to express their doubts. A good way to address the belief ques-tion is to encourage students to ask themselves, "If I really believe this is true, how should I be acting?" When we raise the belief question, and openly consider it, there is a much better chance that our students will embrace spiritual truths and then act on them.

The third question on students' minds follows close on the heels of the second: *So what?* This really is the application question. Once we understand what is being taught and really believe it, then it is a short step to what we should do about it. Until we get to this point in our teaching, we really haven't completed the task before us. Jesus usually was persistent in demanding that His students consider how they acted. And we should do no less. We need to help our students understand spiritual truth, make sure that they really do believe it, and determine how they should act because of what they believe.

TEACHING CHILDREN: Most of the questions that we ask young children will relate to the facts. It is very important that we communicate so that they understand what we are teaching. The second category of questions regarding belief is less critical because younger children are quite open in accepting what we say. But we should always encourage them to consider what they should be doing because of what they have learned.

As children grow older, the second category relating to belief becomes much more important. Elementary age children will begin to question what they are told. And we want to encourage such questioning in class where we can help to guide them into proper answers. Asking penetrating questions, and encouraging our students to ask them of us, will add greatly to our teaching effectiveness.

It is also important to recognize that for young children there is no such category as rhetorical questions. Once when I was teaching early elementary children I asked rhetorically (and quite innocently), "Have you ever had a fight at your house?" Before I could continue, to my horror, one of the children began describing (in graphic detail) a heated argument between her mother and father the night before. In spite of my attempted intervention, we found out who said what, who threw what at whom, and many other lurid details. Since then I have been careful to ask children only those questions that I really want answered.

TEACHING YOUTH AND ADULTS: While all three categories of questions are important with older students, we ought to spend more time than we ordinarily do in considering questions relating to "Do I really believe that?" This is especially true when we are teaching those who learned many Bible truths when they were growing up. Often those truths have become so common to us that we fail to stop and question if we really believe them.

A good way to broach the topic of belief is to move to the third category of questions, "So what?" We might suggest that true belief results in appropriate behavior. Asking how we would act if we truly believed what the Bible says on a given topic can prove to be a very penetrating question. If we are not living according to our beliefs then perhaps we need to move back and question if we really believe what we claim.

All this is not to imply that we ought to ignore the question of understanding. We should always teach in a clear and precise fashion. This is especially true if we are handling new material or difficult concepts. It is important to set an atmosphere of openness and freedom to question. In this way, students will be able to gain maximum value from our instruction, and we will gain feedback for tailoring our presentation to meet their needs.

NINE

High-Touch
Teaching
(Effective Teaching in a High-Tech World)

Insight on Ministry

Recently I was driving to work early in the morning, struggling to get mind and body to begin cooperating. As I neared a four-way stop a bicyclist approached from my left. Since no other cars were in the vicinity, I waited and motioned the bicyclist to proceed, even though I had reached the stop sign first. It was then that I recognized the bicyclist as a good friend, riding to the train station for his commute into Chicago.

His wave and big grin were a welcome and unexpected source of pleasure. Even though we had not communicated verbally, our chance meeting ignited a warm glow that lasted well into the morning.

After work that same day, I went out to run several miles. Not far into the "agony," I heard behind me the sound of another runner gradually closing the distance between us. As I glanced over at the person passing me, we recognized each other. Although not close friends, we ran together for almost a mile chatting about our common interests. When we separated, I was surprised at how fast the time had passed. Communicating with a friend had completely eclipsed the pain of running.

Reflecting back over that day's experiences, I was reminded of what a significant role friends play in our lives, and how appropriate it is to work actively at building and maintaining those important relationships. Perhaps you are better than I at cultivating friendships, but I do know that I need to give it greater attention.

Our great and increasing need for meaningful relationships is one of the ten major directions (or trends) transforming our lives that researcher John Naisbitt discussed in his book *Megatrends* (Warner Books, 1982). This was his pioneering book documenting our society's transition into an age of high technology.

One of the ten major trends affecting our lives is what Naisbitt calls High Tech/High Touch. He contends that the dramatic increase in high technology demands a corresponding increase in attention to cultivating meaningful human relationships. Television, mass marketing, high-tech automobiles, supersonic transportation, and the dominance of computer technology all can be highly depersonalizing. Technology is cold, sophisticated, and insensitive. But our need for personal interaction drives us to seek warm, human contact — high-touch experiences.

We can increase our effectiveness by employing high-touch methods as we teach in Sunday School and other Christian education programs. Obviously there is room for high-tech instruction. We should seek to use instructional videos, computers, overhead projectors, audio cassette players, and other current technology whenever appropriate. But we need to balance these tools with a high-touch approach.

This means selecting strategies that will build meaningful relationships with our students. We teachers would be wise to heed the advice of the long distance telephone company whose commercials encouraged us to "reach out and touch someone." Clearly this is not a physical touch, though there may be an appropriate time for that too. But we can touch learners through support and encouragement — through sympathetic listening. We reach out and touch them through methods that promote interaction with fellow students as well as with us, the teacher. And we promote high-touch by ministering as Christlike teachers — channels of God's love.

Jesus' ministry was high-touch in approach. Rather than remaining aloof, He built close relationships, explaining to His disciples, "You are My friends, if you do what I command you. No longer do I call you slaves; for the slave does not know what his master is doing; but I have called you friends, for all things that I have heard from My Father I have made known to you" (John 15:14-15).

The warmth and vitality of Christ's teaching were felt by the two disciples whom He taught on the Emmaus road following His resurrection. As the two later reviewed the experience in their minds, they expressed, "Were not our hearts burning within us while He was speaking to us on the road, while He was explaining the Scriptures to us?" (Luke 24:32)

The very nature of instruction demands high-touch. When a person teaches as Christ intended, that person shares more than information with a student. Teachers share the essence of who they are — their very beings. "A pupil is not above his teacher; but everyone, after he has been fully trained, will be like his teacher" (Luke 6:40). Instead of teaching by giving information alone, the challenge is "in speech, conduct, love, faith, and purity, show yourself an example of those who believe" (1 Tim. 4:12).

Teaching always involves methods. But *the kinds* of methods that we use determine the outcome in our students' lives. Some methods primarily draw attention to the knowledge and the position of the teacher. Other methods encourage and promote high-touch. The following methods are relationship-builders that help to draw students and teacher together.

Interactive Discussion. In many traditional classes the teacher serves as *the* source of information. This implies that what the teacher does is the really important issue, and that the teacher is responsible for an interesting presentation that maintains student attention. But true discussion is a cooperative search for a solution to a problem. The teacher should pose a legitimate problem and then provide resources for students to use in discovering the solution. The teacher assists as necessary while students work together, getting to know each other and building meaningful relationships. A valuable fringe benefit is that effective discussion maintains a high level of interest.

Personal Illustration. Teachers can share meaningful events from their own lives. Even though illustration traditionally is a teacher-centered method, it still can be high-touch since it reveals a teacher's vulnerability. One caution should be observed: *present balanced illustrations.* Teachers must be careful not to use only those illustrations that put them in a good light. If a teacher shares both successes *and* failures, students will be able to learn through the teacher's example as well as through direct instruction.

Question and Answer. Questions directed to the students, or taken from the students, also help to build relationships. This method has many of the same values as discussion, but is less formal. Questions to students can help to stimulate thinking and draw them into the lesson. But teachers should be sure that the questions they ask are legitimate questions, worthy of being answered. And the teacher who has learned to teach so that questions are raised in the students' minds can get students even more involved. (When taking questions from students, we must be sure never to imply that their questions are thoughtless or inappropriate, even if occasionally they seem to be.)

Informal Activities. Usually we think of teaching as something that we do in the classroom, at a specific time. However, much learning can be done during informal times, in other places. Taking students on a field trip is one type of informal activity. Other possibilities include social times in your home, hiking, going on a picnic, or attending a sporting event. When teacher and students relate in a loosely-structured, relaxed atmosphere, friendships can grow. In fact, some of the most important foundations for formal instruction can occur in the informal context. What you do with your students *outside* the classroom may well determine whether or not you even have a hearing *in* the classroom.

126

Projects/Ministry. While many students are able to handle abstract concepts, others have a much more hands-on learning style. It is extremely valuable for both types of students to actually work on a project that will help them learn and apply truth. Some classes have assumed responsibility for assisting senior adults with housework or home repair. Others minister monthly at a local retirement home. Look for specific ministries you can provide in your church, perhaps duplicating bulletins, maintaining the building, cleaning the church, or staffing the nursery.

One wise teacher of a junior class arranged for all the "early birds" to work on building a model tabernacle. When students had questions about various elements of the project, class members did research. The greatest challenge the teacher faced was to arrive before the first student did, which seemed to be earlier each week. In addition to providing ministry and/or learning opportunities, projects are high-touch experiences. They put teacher and students into close contact and draw them together.

Case Study. Since students often relegate Bible truth to some ancient time period, we need to help them understand that God's Word relates to people living today, in the situations all of us face. By using carefully designed and wisely selected real-life situations in a case study approach, students can sense the Bible's relevancy to twentieth century needs. This method promotes high-touch communication because students not only are dealing with actual people's struggles, but they are working with fellow classmates and the teacher to find workable biblical solutions.

Inductive Study. The final method that we will discuss here is actually an approach to study. Inductive study enables class members to dig into the Scriptures for themselves to discover what God has said. I once ministered to a group of teenagers for some months, to the point where we had established open communication and a high level of trust. We had a high-touch relationship. One evening they expressed the need to understand the Bible better. When I explained inductive study to them, they became very excited, and even agreed to meet at 7 o'clock Saturday mornings to learn more. As we studied together, they personally dug into the Scriptures to discover

127

God's meaning for their lives. And we came to appreciate each other deeply during months of shared study.

In its simplest format, inductive study consists of three steps — observation, interpretation, and application. *Observation* is when we seek to answer the basic question, "What does it *say?*" This involves probing the biblical text with questions, and making observations about the passage. *Interpretation* focuses on the meaning of that text. Often this will involve studying other resources to help answer the question, "What does this passage *mean?*" Finally, *application* answers the question, "What does it mean *to me?*" This is the personal step, when students clearly see that the Word of God speaks to people living today. True inductive study will demand a cooperative effort on the part of teacher and learners. In addition to finding personal meaning for life, teacher and students will be able to relate to each other, supporting and encouraging one another in the process.

Much about our age is cold and impersonal. Many people feel alone, cut off, isolated. And while technology has made many parts of our lives easier, it also has contributed to a sense of alienation. We can provide a healthy balance by including high-touch methods in our Bible teaching. We can assist students in better understanding themselves and each other. High-touch teaching helps to restore a sense of value and dignity to our students. It reminds them that they are God's handiwork, created in His image, people for whom Christ gave Himself. As we teach our students, let's reach out and touch — touch them for Christ.

(For additional help in understanding these and other methods, refer to *24 Ways to Improve Your Teaching* by Kenneth O. Gangel, Victor Books, 1972. A training kit to go with this book, written by Elaine and Wes Willis, also is available, Scripture Press, 1988.)

Insight from the Word (Part One)

The belief that a Christian can function in isolation clearly contradicts New Testament teaching. Several passages describe Christians as members of a body. Christ is the head who gives direction to the body, and each Christian has a unique function as a member of that body. Just as the parts of our physical bodies are interconnected and interdependent, so are the members of the church—the body of Christ.

Each of us is responsible to look for ways that we can support, promote, and encourage others who are in the body. When this happens the body is strong and healthy. But when it does not happen the body is weak and ineffective. This means that every believer ought to be important to us. It is especially important that teachers be faithful to encourage, promote, and support those whom they teach. If one of our students is hurting, we should share that person's pain as fellow members of the body. Part of a teacher's responsibility is to seek out ways to build meaningful relationships with students so that they can be strong and vital members of the body of Christ.

Read Galatians 6:2-5. Notice that there are two statements that seem to contradict each other in this passage. Verse 2 exhorts us to carry each other's burdens, and then verse 5 challenges each of us to carry his own load. The words that have been translated burdens (v. 2) and load (v. 5) come from two different Greek words. "Burdens" (v. 2) comes from a word meaning a heavy, crushing load that is more than one person could carry alone. "Load" (v. 5) comes from the same root word that Christ used in Matthew 11:30 where He described the burden of discipleship that each of His followers should bear. How are these two concepts complementary rather than contradictory? _____

_____

_____

What kinds of crushing loads might a fellow Christian need help to carry? _____

_____

In what ways do you think one Christian can help another who is carrying that sort of a crushing load? _____

_____

_____

What is the reason Paul gave to explain why we ought to help others who need help? (v. 2) _____

_____

Read John 13:34. How does this law of Christ help to illuminate Paul's instructions in Galatians 6:2? _____

_____

_____

How does Galatians 6:3 serve to remind us that we are not self-sufficient?

_____

_____

Since verse 5 refers to our individual responsibility to live as followers of Jesus Christ, why is it important that we evaluate our own actions and not try to compare ourselves with others? (v. 4) _____

_____

_____

Identify strategies to maintain a proper balance between helping others carry their loads and humbly carrying your own responsibility to live as Christ's disciple. _____

_____

_____

_____

Read 2 Corinthians 1:3-7 to discover another place where Paul wrote about believers encouraging each other. What are two titles used to describe God in this passage? (v. 3) _____

_____

_____

What ministry does God provide to us who are believers? (v. 4)

_____

And then how are we enabled to help others since we have been helped by God? (v. 4) _____

_____

_____

How should the sufferings that Christ experienced influence Christians who are living today? (v. 5) _____

_____

_____

In what ways are all believers inseparably bound so that none of us functions in isolation? (vv. 6-7) _____

_____

_____

Insight from the Word (Part Two)

In teaching we can approach our students in many different ways. One common approach is to focus primarily on the content that must be learned. Teachers who approach their ministry from this perspective tend to be well prepared and have a high sense of the Bible's importance. They know what they want to communicate and they work hard at sharing what they have prepared. Unfortunately, such teachers may not be very approachable. Sometimes they seem to be cold and aloof. They may not feel that they are that way at all. But if their primary emphasis is "covering the material," then their focus on sharing facts may not contribute to building personal relationships with students.

At the other extreme is the Sunday School teacher who is vitally concerned with relating to his or her students. Such a teacher may concentrate so much on relationship-building that the Scriptures may be neglected. Although the students learn little from the Bible, they certainly do enjoy their time together. Teachers taking this type of approach employ methods that are extremely relational.

The key to effective biblical teaching is avoiding either extreme — to be neither totally content nor totally student oriented. We must teach the facts and the principles of the Word. And we must also build meaningful relationships with students. Authoritative and approachable should describe our teaching style. While giving valid attention to the content we also can utilize methods that encourage interaction and relationship building.

Read Mark 11:27-33. How did Jesus give those whom He was teaching the freedom to discuss and interact with Him? ____

_____

_____

_____

How did He confront them with the importance of thinking through difficult issues while honestly struggling to understand truth? _____

_____

_____

_____

Read Matthew 9:35-38. How do the qualities of concern and sensitivity balance with Jesus' authority and affirmation of truth?

_____

_____

Scan through chapters 8 to 10 of the Gospel of Mark. Write down the various ways in which Jesus established relationships through communicating with those whom He taught. _____

_____

_____

_____

_____

_____

_____

List some of the principles that could help to guide you in your teaching as you work at balancing the emphasis on authoritative content with personal concern for your students. _____

133

_____

_____

_____

_____

_____

_____

_____

_____

Insight on Teaching

TEACHING CHILDREN: Those who teach children often find it a very gratifying experience. Preschoolers are delighted when they happen to meet their teachers outside of class. Often early school-age children will come to Sunday School long before starting time so as not to be late. And they are gravely disappointed if the teacher is not there. Later school-age children are open and responsive to their teacher, enjoying the informal times of talking together.

There are several ways that a teacher can build on such dynamics. Obviously a teacher needs to talk to his or her students. One of the best times to do this is before class begins. As each child arrives, talk informally about what has been happening in that child's world. Unfortunately, sometimes the teacher is one of the last to arrive. Or the teacher may be present but preparing for class or talking to other teachers and ignoring the children. Teachers should try to arrive before the first student and use that time wisely to communicate with the children.

Guided conversation is an excellent method to build quality relationships even as you are teaching. Many curriculum materials will suggest ways to incorporate guided conversation into the lesson. It consists of "talking through the lesson" rather than "presenting the lesson." It permits flexibility and interaction in class; both teachers and students appreciate this. Other effective approaches which provide for building relationships and student/teacher interaction include question and answer and storytelling.

TEACHING YOUTH: High-touch teaching not only is *helpful* in ministering to youth, it is *imperative.* The world is full of people trying to "sell" something to teens. Whether it is advertisers trying to market the latest craze or those in authority trying to get them to behave, teens are bombarded with instructions. In some instances young people choose to assert independence, reacting the opposite of what is desired. In other cases, they are taken in and buy into the message without evaluating its content. Either reaction is bad.

We teachers need to break through the clutter of our age. But we can't do this by yelling louder or out-promoting "Madison Avenue." Instead, we ought to build quality relationships — concentrate on high-touch teaching. We must listen to what our youth think and feel in a noncritical, nonjudgmental manner. Talk about the things that interest them. Find out what they worry about. Pay attention to their concerns. Then draw on these discoveries to illustrate Bible truths at a later time. In the final analysis, the actual methods that you use are less important than conveying a genuine concern for, and sincere interest in, your students. They will survive, and even thrive, on average quality teaching if they know that you really care for them as individuals.

TEACHING ADULTS: Many adults feel as though their lives consist of one crisis after another linked together by a combination of exhaustion and anxiety. And some church programs take an already complicated life and tangle it still further with programs, activities, and demands on time. But Sunday School can provide a respite.

Obviously the class period can be a time of building relationships. But beyond this, Sunday School offers the possibility of relating with a small number of genuinely concerned friends. Small classes are ideal fellowship/support groups. Large classes can subdivide into groups of ten to fifteen adults for mutual caring and support. My wife and I were in a very large Sunday School class that formed smaller sharing groups. Six couples who expressed an interest in serious Bible study and sharing were assigned to a small group. We have been meeting for a number of years now, and we find that these are some of our closest friends in the church. In the midst of a high-tech world, we have a high-touch Bible study group.

Look for ways to get adults into small enough groups so that they can develop meaningful personal relationships and encourage each other. This will not only strengthen them personally, but it will help them to grow and mature into positions of leadership within the church.

EPILOGUE

The person who I am today is the product of many forces at work in my life over the years. My parents, my two brothers (one older, one younger), and many other relatives have had a hand in my development. Friends, neighbors, and other acquaintances played a part too. Opportunities and circumstances, both in early years and then later in life, contributed greatly. School, work, and church experiences added their unique contributions. When all of these, plus countless others, are factored into one complex mathematical equation and modified by my unique genetic structure, the result is what I am.

Since the focus of this book is developing a unique teaching approach, it would be profitable to recall some meaningful Christian education experiences. The first teacher who comes to mind is an early elementary Sunday School teacher. Mrs. Harvey Hiles, now with the Lord, taught and loved me. I'm sure that she prepared well, used good methods, and derived maximum value from the curriculum resources that she had available. But those are not the things that I recall. The thing that I remember is loving, gentle acceptance. She loved me, and I knew it.

The next teacher who comes to mind taught me in the junior department. Actually, I feel somewhat guilty when I think about those years in Sunday School. J. Rollin Ewen had been assigned a formidable task. Any professional teacher could have changed vocations after a tour of duty (perhaps it was more like a sentence) with our class. The other boys were horribly uncooperative. They misbehaved regularly, and rather than using their creativity to learn God's Word, they constantly devised new and terrible ways to afflict Mr. Ewen. It's funny that I can't remember myself misbehaving in that class. It must have been the other boys—very strange. And while obviously there were many things that we didn't learn, one thing we did know. We knew that Mr. Ewen really cared for us. He had to care, to put up with what we (I mean "they") did.

The next teacher I recall was far more than my Junior High Sunday School teacher. He also was my pastor. Rev. James N. McCoy tried to do something with us that would contribute to our spiritual growth and development. And he probably thought that he didn't accomplish much. But he did. He helped to instill a deep appreciation for God's Word and for the importance of the church, the body of Christ. It didn't seem strange to us then to have our pastor serving as our Sunday School teacher; but as I travel around the country, rarely do I find a Senior Pastor (he was our *only* pastor) who also is willing to serve as a Junior High Sunday School teacher.

I could go on and list other teachers who have made vital contributions in my life. As I think back through college, seminary, graduate school, and beyond, many teachers could be commemorated in *my* "Teacher Hall of Fame." Some of them were outstanding—true artisans of the teaching craft who used all of the right methods, and used them effectively. Others were far less skilled, perhaps doing some wrong things, but usually for the right reasons. But all of them have made a lasting imprint on my life—they are part of the equation. As godly men and women, willing to serve unsung and often unappreciated, they continue to influence me today. They are a vital and eternal part of who and what I am. They served God by serving me as my teachers.

God has called each of us to serve Him. As teachers, we should feel a deep obligation to prepare and to teach to the best of our abilities. God has entrusted us with His Word, the truth that the Apostle Paul described as the secret things of God. "So then, men ought to regard us as servants of Christ and as those entrusted with the secret things of God. Now it is required that those who have been given a trust must prove faithful" (1 Cor. 4:1-2, NIV). Faithful teachers are those who love and obey our Saviour Jesus Christ. And they communicate this love through who and what they are, even more than by what they do. It is important that we be people who truly love Christ. And then as faithful servants we will allow His love to reach out through us to our students.

In all probability most of your students never will report to you the impact you had in their lives. Indeed, they may not even be aware of it themselves. But God knows when we are faithful. And what really matters is not whether our students or anyone else knows what we have done. What finally matters is that we be commemorated in God's "Teacher Hall of Fame."